Real Evangelistic Preaching

REAL EVANGELISTIC PREACHING

Bailey E. Smith

BROADMAN PRESS
Nashville, Tennessee

4262-29

ISBN: 0-8054-6229-5

Dewey Decimal Classification: 252.3

Subject heading: EVANGELISTIC SERMONS

Library of Congress Catalog Card Number: 80-70913

Printed in the United States of America

Contents

1
Nothing Succeeds Like Failure

In Galatians 6:7-9 we read, "For whatsoever a man soweth, that shall he also reap. For he that soweth to his flesh shall of the flesh reap corruption; but he that soweth to the Spirit shall of the Spirit reap life everlasting. And let us not be weary in well doing: for in due season we shall reap, if we faint not."

We have heard the following statement all of our lives. *Nothing* succeeds like success. Now to a certain degree, this is true. Crowds engender crowds. Enthusiasm builds enthusiasm.

The other side is that negativism breeds negativism. I mean, you can get around folks that are down in the dumps, and pretty soon you, too, are in the dumps. Consequently, there are some folks I try to avoid. You talk about what a beautiful day it is and they say, "Yes, but I'll bet there's a cloud somewhere." They always have a negative attitude.

I love people that are positive. There are a few folks I love because I've never known them to be negative. They are always positive. They always see the good side of every situation. That is a wonderful and valuable character trait. *Nothing succeeds like success.*

But, listen carefully. I want us to examine this statement: Nothing succeeds like failure. If you want to know something that will produce a harvest, year after year, it is failure. Failure is like throwing a rock into the ocean or into a pond. It will gather ever-broadening circles of

7

influence. Like a pebble in a pool, the ripples grow. And a man who fails has an influence upon life and will touch harvest after harvest. Nothing succeeds like failure. Failure is extremely fruitful.

I remember a young friend of mine. When we were in school, we used to go across the campus at lunch to eat. We would go in a store and I'd get a big sour pickle and a pineapple fried pie and an RC Cola. (That explains my disposition, doesn't it?) Well, my friend, Bill, had a problem with stealing things. He would go up to the bubble gum counter and take a few pieces of bubble gum. Sometimes he would take a package of potato chips. They would fit so neatly under his shirt.

In the wintertime when we wore coats, Bill would really get blessed. When he had his coat on, he could hide more. Well, I got a letter from Bill not too long ago. It came from El Reno Prison. I should have known. You see, just a little bit of failure, a little bit of sin, will grow and grow until a person develops criminal tendencies. I'm telling you, one of the most fruitful things in life is failure. Yes, failure.

And, to add to that, not only is it the things we do, but so often it is the things we don't do. Friends, a man is going to harvest whatever he plants. We cannot hope to plant brier seeds and harvest corn. We cannot expect to neglect an area of land and have it sprout forth fruit. I've got an area of land in my backyard that I have neglected and there is nothing there I want to eat. I've not grown any peas, okra, squash, or tomatoes on that area of land that I've neglected. Sometimes we neglect our souls; we neglect our lives; we neglect our bodies; these failures bring regrettable results. The sin of omission is as bad as the sin of commission.

A man once asked a little boy, "Son, do you know

what the sins of omission are?" The lad said, "I certainly
do." Surprised, the man said, "Well, what are they?"
The boy said, "Mister, that's those sins we ought to be
doing and we're not." Many folks may interpret sins of
omission like that. This chapter will address this type of
failure.

Let's look at five fruitful failures. For many of you,
these will penetrate your hearts, and I hope will stir
your souls. And for many of you, they could bring about
a total change in your lives. The Bible speaks of five
fruitful failures. These are all failures that brought forth
fruit.

When You Sow Disobedience, You Reap Destruction

The first failure is found in Daniel 5:1-4. Listen carefully to the principle. When you sow disobedience, you
reap destruction. How many of you really believe the
biblical teaching that whatever you sow you shall also
reap? Really? Do you believe that? Most would say,
"Sure!" However, if some of you were to harvest right
now what you are planting morally, you would reap
embarrassment. If some of you were to harvest what
you're planting in your home, you would reap divorce.

In Daniel 5:1-4 we find the story of Belshazzar. "Belshazzar the king made a great feast to a thousand of his
lords, and drank wine before the thousand. Belshazzar,
while he tasted the wine, commanded [Now, folks, this
was the thing that literally 'undid' him before the Lord]
to bring the golden and silver vessels which his father
Nebuchadnezzar had taken out of the temple which was
in Jerusalem; that the king, and his princes, his wives,
and his concubines, might drink therein. [He was really
going to be the 'big daddy' of the night, wasn't he?] Then
they brought the golden vessels that were taken out of

the temple of the house of God which was at Jerusalem
[notice the progress of sin]; and the king, and his
princes, his wives, and his concubines, drank in them.
They drank wine, and praised the gods of gold, and of
silver, of brass, of iron, of wood, and of stone."
     Let's stop here for just a moment. The scene is a beau-
tiful, gorgeous night. I can just see those hanging gardens of Babylon. I can almost smell the fragrance of the
imported flowers brought there to appease the mighty
guests that would come. And look at Belshazzar. The son
of Nebuchadnezzar is sitting on this throne, looking at
those beautiful hanging gardens of Babylon. I'm sure the
Oriental birds were singing. Those elegant fountains
were showering their spray, and the breeze was blowing
the water refreshingly into the face of Belshazzar and
his guests. The dancing girls came by in their flimsy
garments to entertain the thousand lords that had come
that day for the big party of Belshazzar as he claimed
victory over all the land. Not only was Belshazzar feeling pleasure, but he felt secure because through that
Babylonian empire meandered the great Euphrates
River. He was protected. He was also protected by walls
that were 350 feet high and 86 feet thick. Not only was
he protected by the meandering Euphrates River and by
those walls 350 feet high and 86 feet thick, but, also soldiers stood guard to protect the mighty king, Belshazzar.
     He began to feel a little bit arrogant and cocky, so he
said to his lords, "You know that time we stole the vessels from the Temple? Bring in those golden vessels."
And they brought in the golden vessels and he went
over and uncorked the wine, and began pouring the wine
into those vessels.
     I can see that dirty, filthy king's saliva flowing down

his mouth, and dribbling down his clothing. He reached down and grabbed the golden vessel and he said, "Ha, ha, ha, look at that. That used to be used in the house of God! Ha! They call it communion. Look at it! Look at it, friends, look at it! Something that used to be used in the service of the Lord! Ha, ha, look at that!" And then he took the alcohol to his lips and he drank. Then he passed the golden vessels around. He said, "You harlots, you concubines, you wives of mine, you drink out of these golden vessels, too. It's going to be a great party tonight. The golden vessels of the Lord, dedicated tonight to the wonderful love for Belshazzar."

Pretty soon the music stopped. A messenger ran to Belshazzar and said, "Belshazzar, Darius has already broken through the wall." Belshazzar said, "It's a lie!" "No," said the guard, "Darius and the Medes, the whole army of the Medes are here. Belshazzar, listen to us!" "Ha," he said, "dance some more, girls. Take off a few more garments, girls. Hey, lords, didn't I provide a good party tonight for you? Man, look at that third one. Isn't she something? Wow! A little more wine, please."

Well, the arrogant Belshazzar was having a great time. But, pretty soon Darius and the Medes rushed into the magnificent palace. They thrust a sword into the heart of the king. They took the women and killed them, also. The blood flowed from Belshazzar and mixed with the wine and saliva and perspiration, and flowed down the marble steps of that palace as Belshazzar met his death.

You see, God had written on those chalky white walls of Babylon, "Mene, Mene, Tekel, Upharsin" (Dan. 5:25), which literally means that Belshazzar had been weighed on God's scales and found to be wanting. My friend, when you sow disobedience, you reap destruction. It always happens.

Now, think about something. In this time the golden vessel of the Lord is your body. Many people, like Belshazzar, say, "Ha! My body dedicated to the service of the Lord, the temple of the Holy Spirit. Bring me my body. I want to fill it up. I'm going to fill it with pleasure." So we smoke it up. If you could take some folks and turn them wrong-side out, they'd look like a charcoal grill. We want to smoke it up. We want to drink it up. We are going to dope it up. My friend, when you sow disobedience to your body, you destroy your body. Is that clear enough? When you disobey God concerning your soul, you destroy your soul. When you disobey God in your mind, you destroy your emotions. When a man sows disobedience, he reaps destruction. It will never fail.

I once visited a forty-six-year-old man in the hospital. He was dying of cancer. I have since that time preached the funeral of that dear man. As he was dying, he was coughing and hacking in a terrible way. His lungs were literally eaten up by over twenty years of smoking. He reached with his trembling hands to a package of cigarettes. As I watched, he picked up that cigarette package, got a cigarette out, and just as he was about to put it to his lips, he held the cigarette over by a picture of his family. It was a picture of his daughter, son, and wife that he was about to leave in early death. He held that cigarette up by the picture and over and over he said as he looked at me, "Preacher it's not worth it, is it? It's just not worth it." I replied, "No, sir, it wouldn't be for me."

It's not worth it. My friend, when you laugh at the fact that the Christian's body is the temple of the Holy Spirit, and make fun of it, and disobey God's laws about the body, you will destroy the body. You will destroy the soul. You will destroy the mind. When disobedience comes, destruction always follows.

How many men have died early because they disobeyed God? We live all tensed up. Somebody says hello to us and we say, "What did he mean by that? What does he want from me?" We get angry and cantankerous, and then blame it on our schedule. You know what I've learned? There's time enough in every day to do what God wants you to do, with a sweet spirit. I do not mean to include all of the junk you throw in your day that God had nothing to do with. But, there is enough time in every day to do what God wants us to do. We don't have to be tense.

Some folks dope it up. I was talking to a person recently who was telling me about all the dope he had been on. I said, "How's it been?" He replied, "Well, man, while I did it, it was really fun." I asked, "You really enjoyed it?" He said, "I couldn't see straight, walk straight, or think straight." I thought to myself, *Why would anyone think Christianity is based on shallow emotionalism*? My dear friend, the most intelligent, wonderful thing one can ever do is give his heart to Jesus Christ. Jesus won't wreck your body. He won't wreck your emotions. He won't wreck your soul. Belshazzar had to learn the hard way that when a man turns his eyes off God, he has put himself against God. That man had better be careful.

So many churches fall into this trap. They begin to worship form, and they reap deadness. They begin to sow culture, and they reap meaningless worship. Have any of you disobeyed God? My friends, if you've disobeyed God physically, emotionally, or mentally, please repent and return to rest and peace in Jesus. Doctors have told me for years that 50 percent to 60 percent of the people that they examine in hospital beds are not organically sick. They are emotionally and mentally ill because they have disobeyed God and his laws and have suffered the consequences.

When You Sow Looseness, You Reap Loneliness

The second fruitful failure is kindred to the first. In 1 Samuel 15:21-27 we find the story of Saul. "But the people took of the spoil, sheep and oxen, the chief of the things which should have been utterly destroyed, to sacrifice unto the Lord thy God in Gilgal (v. 21). Now, Saul had disobeyed God. God told him not to do that. "And Samuel said unto Saul, I will not return with thee: [They were the dearest friends; Samuel being the preacher and Saul being the king.] for thou hast rejected the word of the Lord, and the Lord hath rejected thee from being king over Israel. And as Samuel turned about to go away, he laid hold upon the skirt of his mantle, and it rent" (vv. 26-27). He did this in grief and despair over what Saul had done. Samuel left! When you live loosely, you reap loneliness.

Every now and then someone will say to me, "Brother Bailey, I've been saved. Since then my drinking buddies and cussing buddies and dope buddies don't want to be around me anymore. What am I going to do?" Well, guess what? Any friendship you have to give up in order to receive Jesus Christ as Savior, you didn't need in the first place. If your friendship with someone is based upon how often you have sex, how much liquor you drink, how often you go to X-rated movies, how much pot you smoke, ad infinitum, my friend, that's not a friendship. That's simply a contract made with hell itself. You don't need that kind of friendship. You'd best listen up! When a man has had "some kind" of relationship with Christ, and begins to turn against the things that are holy and righteous, and begins to live loosely toward the things in the Bible, watch out!

I know a preacher right now who's lonely. Once he preached to crowds larger than I'll ever preach to, but, he began to look at a little blonde, a little brunette, and a little redhead, a little go-go girl. Finally his wife found out about it. His son-in-law who worked for him found out about it. And now that man is an embarrassment to himself and a disgrace to God. He and his wife are divorced and will probably never be back together. The man is crying out, "Oh, if I had some Christian friends." He is lonely! When you begin to take the standards of God loosely, it's going to bring loneliness.

Saul made the mistake of thinking that God would compromise his standard. He said to himself, "I know what God said, but, I believe that deep down in God's heart he really doesn't care if I do this." My friend, don't be loose about interpreting the Bible. Looseness brings loneliness.

I received a letter sometime ago from a prisoner in a Florida prison. The young man wrote: "I am waiting to be executed. Thank you very much for writing me. I have been saved, but I don't know the exact date. I don't know anyone at this time who is interested in the prison ministry. I would like to correspond with anyone who is interested in writing to me. I have been here on death row one year. I would like to tell you a few things about myself. My IQ is 155. I graduated from high school at the age of fourteen. I completed three years at the University of Southern California. I served in the Vietnam war, and I was in the Air Force three years, ten months, forty-two and one-half minutes. I'm an ex-policeman from Miami, Florida. Anybody on this earth, no matter who he is, can commit a crime. I did, and I am guilty. I would appreciate it very much if someone at the First Southern Baptist Church would correspond with me. Yours truly, _____." There's a lonely man, a man who began to loosely interpret the things of God, the things of righteousness, the things of holiness, and the Ten Commandments. It led him to loneliness.

A wife who had lost her family said to me, "Preacher, for twenty years of marriage I was not a scriptural wife and finally my husband said, 'I've had enough of you. I've had enough of your coldness, your deadness, of your distance to me as my wife. I need someone who will be affectionate to me. You and the kids can do what you want. I want to find a woman who will love me.' " She said, "Preacher, I've been a fool." Now, listen, I'm not justifying that man. He was wrong. He was dead wrong. But what I am saying is when you begin to take any part of the Word of God and interpret it loosely, it will lead to loneliness.

Many people are alone tonight because they didn't stick to the Book. Saul's best friend, Samuel, looked at him and said, "Saul, I'll be seeing you. I can no longer fellowship with you."

You say, "Preacher, I really feel some things are right for me and maybe not right for you." Ah, I've heard that all my life! Listen, you can rest assured that someone who says that has got a little "hanky-panky" going on somewhere. He says, "I know what's right for you may not be right for me," and vice versa. Let me tell you something, friend, if it's wrong for you, it's wrong for me! And if it's wrong for me, it's wrong for you! You say, "Well, Preacher, it depends on the situation." The situation does not determine right or wrong. The Bible determines right or wrong.

Still others say, "Well, Preacher, don't you believe in the statement 'Let your conscience be your guide!' " No! I believe, "Let the Bible be your guide." Some folks have consciences I wouldn't trust with King Kong. You see, it's not your conscience that should be your guide. It must be the Bible. I don't even trust my own conscience. Even though my life has been essentially and relatively right and pure, I sometimes have to seek the Word of God on special issues and say, "God, I don't trust my own judgment. What do *you* have to say about it?" The Word is our guide. Any looseness in that thought will lead to loneliness.

Dr. Bill Hogue, director of evangelism for the Home Mission Board of the Southern Baptist Convention, was eating dinner with another fellow in Philadelphia. As they were eating, two young girls came up to them, sat down beside the men, and said, "Hello."

Bill Hogue said, "Hello." Then the two girls grinned at each other and said, "We're hookers."

Dr. Hogue replied, "Well, that's interesting." At this point they began to offer their services to Dr. Hogue and his companion. Bill said, "Well, you see, I really wouldn't be interested in that because I'm a Baptist preacher."

One of the girls said, "Well, great! I'm a Baptist, too."

He said, "Really? Let me ask you something, Baptist girl. After you spend a day turning tricks, and you get back to your apartment, shut the door, and stand there by yourself, what do you feel like?"

Dr. Hogue said the girl looked stunned as she replied, "You know, I feel two things. Every night when I go home after a day of doing what I do, I feel that I'll die in the night. I feel for some reason that I'm going to die, and I'm not ready to. Next, I feel so lonely. You cannot imagine how lonely I feel. When my day of prostitution is over, I feel so lonesome that I want to run away." My friend, looseness brings loneliness.

I was on an airplane several months ago and sat by a man who was wearing a clerical collar. We began to talk and I found he was a minister of another denomination. The stewardess came by, as they always do, saying, "Cocktail, cocktail." I don't know why the boozers get waited on first. They never come by first saying, "Dr. Pepper, Dr. Pepper." The stewardess came by and said to me, "Cocktail?" I wanted to give her the clever answer a friend of mine always uses. When the stewardess asks him if he wants a cocktail, he answers, "No, thank you. The feathers tickle my throat."

Well, the stewardess looked like she'd had a bad day, so I said, "No, Ma'am." Now, I thought I was going to have a spiritual conversation with the man, but to my surprise, he said, "Yes, I believe I'll have a Bloody Mary." Well, he had a Bloody Mary, and he had Bloody Mary, Jr., and Bloody Mary the third. I said, "You know, I haven't told you who I am. I'm a Baptist preacher." And he said, "Yes, I figured as much." I said, "You know Baptists don't believe in alcohol." He said, "Well, you Baptists are narrow!" I said, "Yes, Sir, but you're compromising." He said, "Man, I'm not compromising. I'm just more liberal."

Listen to me carefully. When it comes to the Bible, there is no such thing as liberalism and conservatism. The difference is between the truth and a lie. If you take the Bible and expand it, and expand it, and expand it, big enough to fit all of your idiosyncrasies, you've made the truth a lie. God's Word was never meant to be elastic in order to fit around the size of your soul or your heart.

The Bible is what it is. We must not have the Bible bend to us. We are to bend to the Bible.

It is interesting to me that as Belshazzar began to worship the gods of gold, of silver, and of brass, God wouldn't allow it. Don't you find it interesting that when God wouldn't let him do what he wanted to do, he just found another god? That's what America is doing. We want to go to a church that believes like we believe. Try something for me. Why don't you go to a church that believes what God believes. I frequently hear this little phrase, "Go to the church of your choice." Baloney! Go to the church of God's choice. If you are in a church that's not preaching the Bible, the blood, and the blessed hope, you'd better get out of that church so fast they'll think you were raptured. I'm being serious with you. Life is short. If you're in a church that dilutes the Bible, leave it. Leave it! Remember this second failure: Looseness brings loneliness.

When You Sow Sin, You Reap Suffering

When you sow disobedience, you will reap destruction. When you sow looseness, you will reap loneliness. Let us now examine the third fruitful failure. When you sow sin, you will reap suffering.

The story of Samson in Judges 16 is a very clear picture of sin and suffering. Delilah woke Samson crying, "The Philistines be upon thee, Samson" (v. 20). He awoke out of his sleep and the Lord had departed from him. I think this is one of the saddest verses I've ever read in the Bible. Wouldn't it be an awful thing to lead singing or to preach and not even know the Lord wasn't with you? Wouldn't it be horrible?

The Philistines took Samson and blinded him. They brought him down to Gaza and bound him with fetters of brass. Man, that's sad to me. Here was a man of God. Here was a man that was strong. One time he was tied to the beams of a wall, and he just pulled the entire wall down. That's how strong he was. One time he captured a bunch of foxes. He tied their tails together, set them on fire, sent them through the corn patch, and burned down the Philistines' corn. Now, it takes a pretty smart fellow to do that, doesn't it?

I'd like to have known a man like that. I admire men who are physically strong. To me there is something that is good about a man who takes care of himself physically. Oh, but Samson was a man who was unbelievably strong. The Philistines would bind him with all kinds of cords, chains, and fetters, and Delilah would say, "Samson, the Philistines be upon thee." And he'd flex his triceps and biceps and burst the chains and fetters and new ropes. Then he'd go out and literally kill the Philistines who did it. One time he took the jawbone of an animal and killed a thousand Philistines. He just slew them. Oh! It must have been unbelievable. It'd be hard to do that with a machine gun, and he did it with a bone. What a man!

But wait! What happened to him? One prostitute, one harlot, one lie to God, and pretty soon the strong man became weak. A man of God became a man of sin. A holy man became an unholy man. Why did the difference come? The difference came because sin entered the picture. And sin leads to suffering.

It's amazing how many people have the answers for everyone else's problems, and can't even straighten out their own. Here was a man who could destroy a corn patch with fire, but he couldn't put out the fire of lust in his own soul. Here was a man who could break the physical fetters that were wrapped around him, but he couldn't break the shackles of sin that were making his own immoral thoughts captive. Isn't it amazing how folks are always wonderfully aware of your problems but can't take care of their own?

Oh, Samson. Didn't you know that sin leads to suffering? They took him. They bound him. They blinded him. Then they put him at the mill to grind like an ox. How true it is that sin binds, and blinds, and grinds. Sin brings suffering. For an example, go into an orphanage. Why do you think most of the kids are there? The answer is sin. Just go to most hospital emergency rooms. Most of the people are in those rooms because of sin. If a person sows sin, the Bible says he will reap suffering.

Some of you are flirting with sin right now. Caution! Your sin is going to bring suffering. It's happened thousands of times over. All of my life I've preached to people who flirt with sin. I've preached to them in various pastorates, and I thought they were living on a lofty plane. But, all of a sudden, a skeleton would come dancing out of the closet of the past, and they'd say, "Oh, Preacher, I never told you that I indulged in this little pleasure." Beware! Sin brings suffering.

When You Sow Jealousy, You Reap Judgment

The fourth fruitful failure is found in Genesis 4:11. If you sow jealousy, you will reap judgment. In Genesis 4:11 we find another classic illustration in the story of Cain and Abel. What was really wrong with Cain? Well, let's look at the climax. "And now art thou cursed from the earth, which hath opened her mouth to receive thy brother's blood from thy hand." Cain was a vegetable grower, and offered these vegetables as a sacrifice to God. But Abel offered a lamb. God came and literally licked up the sacrifice of Abel with a fire, but he left Cain's offering alone. God's action made Cain jealous.

How many folks are like that? They'd like to eliminate Baptists sometimes because Baptists have been successful in some areas. This is simply jealousy. They say, "Well, I know what you Baptists teach, but I want to do it my way." My friend, Cain did it his way and it made a murderer out of him. He was jealous of God's blessings upon someone else.

When a man does it his way, he's going to wind up in hell. What tragedy that a person will actually desire to do what Cain did. Cain did it his way, and it brought death. Some of you say, "Well, Preacher, I don't care what you say about faith, I still believe you get to heaven by works." Well, listen to Ephesians 2:8-9. "For by grace are ye saved through faith; and that not of yourselves: it is the gift of God: Not of works, lest any man should boast." You say, "Preacher, I just don't care what you say. I don't believe there's a hell." My friend, Revelation 21:8 teaches that all the unbelieving, the whoremongers, the liars, the adulterers, will be cast into a lake which burneth with fire and brimstone. You see, however you try to change it, jealousy brings judgment. God's Word is true and faithful. It is also the last word.

When You Sow Hardness, You Reap Heartache

For the fifth and final fruitful failure, we will look at Exodus 4:21-23. Here we see that if you sow hardness, you will reap heartache. "And the Lord said unto Moses, When thou goest to return into Egypt, see that thou do all those wonders before Pharaoh, which I have put in thine hand: but I will harden his heart, that he shall not let the people go. And thou shalt say unto Pharaoh,

Thus saith the Lord, Israel is my son, even my firstborn:
And I say unto thee, Let my son go, that he may serve
me: and if thou refuse to let him go, behold, I will slay
thy son, even thy firstborn."

Now, let me ask you something. Did Pharaoh harden
his heart? The answer is yes. Did his son get killed? Yes,
he did. Listen carefully—when you sow hardness, you
will reap heartache. Pharaoh came in that night and
found the dead body of his oldest son, and he screamed,
"How could this happen? My son! My firstborn!"

Obviously, Pharaoh didn't know that what happened
didn't just happen that night. It happened back when he
hardened his heart against God. It really happened
when he planted the seed. The death of his son was
merely the harvest. Some of us have gone to funerals
where killing was done way back when the deceased disobeyed almighty God.

Please hear this! When you harden your heart against
the Word of God, heartache follows. I've had people
blame God for some terrible things that happened to
them. "Why did God let that happen to me?" they ask. "I
don't want to serve a God like that." They begin to get
bitter and harden their heart. Don't get stiff against a
Holy God. He knows how to take you and crumble you.
Don't bow your neck against God. Don't harden your
heart against God. Heartache will follow.

You retort, "Well, he couldn't do anything worse to
me than this." Don't kid yourself. When Pharaoh hardened his heart, the Bible says heartache came sweeping
in.

I often hear the question, "Well, why did God harden
Pharaoh's heart?" Listen to the explanation of that. God
did not say, "Pharaoh, I want your heart to be hard. So
there—it's hard!" You see, it was the existence of God

that hardened his heart. I mean the very *fact* of God hardened his heart. God didn't want his heart to be hard. Pharaoh would have been fine if God had left him alone and said, "Pharaoh, you do whatever you want to with my people. I really don't care. Pharaoh, you have your own way."

For example, my preaching has hardened some hearts. I didn't harden their heart, but the existence of preaching did. You see, God didn't intentionally harden Pharaoh's heart, but the very fact that God existed and God has principles did it.

I walked up to the door of a house the other day with a friend of mine and mentioned that we were from First Southern, and at the very thought of God, the door was slammed! I didn't harden that person's heart, but my presence did. And the presence of God hardened Pharaoh's heart because everything God was for, Pharaoh was against.

My friend, do you know why I can preach with all of my energy out of love for you time after time and some of you become angry and rebellious? It's because God's standards cut against the grain of your life-style, your habits, your plans for the future, and you don't like that. It is not Bailey Smith that does it; it is your resistance against the truth. The same sun that melts snow, hardens clay. It all depends on what you're made of. When you get hardened against the preacher or preaching of God's Word, beware—heartache is around the corner.

Pharaoh's heart was hardened and it brought heartache. Some of you don't even have voices worth listening to anymore because of your rebellious spirits. God has told some of you to teach. You have said, "No, God, I'm going to harden myself against that." My friend, heartache is around the corner when you see little children that don't come to Sunday School because nobody is there to teach them. Hardness brings heartache. Some would say, "God, I know you've called me to preach, but no! No! No! No! I'm not going to be a preacher. I'm not going to be a music director. No, God. No!" Oh, listen, that will bring heartache. I know a lot of men selling insurance and cutting hair in barbershops that ought to be preaching. They hardened their hearts and have had one experience of heartache after another. When you sow hardness, you reap heartache.

I don't want to approach God with a hard heart, do you? I pray that you experience the Scripture's power. Remember! Think! "Whatsoever a man soweth, that shall he also reap." What are you sowing? I promise you this, whatever it is, one day you'll harvest it!

2
Seven Kinds of People
God Will Not Save

According to the Scriptures, there are three things necessary for salvation. The first is to *repent* once. Isaiah 55:6 instructs us to seek the Lord while he may be found. This passage indicates that he may not always be available. He may not always be as accessible as he is at other times.

The second is to *believe* or have faith. Acts 16:31 is clear in teaching us that we must *believe* on the Lord Jesus Christ and we shall be saved. Also, John 3:16, "For God so loved the world, that he gave his only begotten Son, that whosoever believeth in him should not perish, but have everlasting life."

Third, we are to *confess*. Romans 10:9 proclaims, "That if thou shalt confess with thy mouth the Lord Jesus, and shalt believe in thine heart that God hath raised him from the dead, thou shalt be saved."

These three ingredients are absolutely necessary for salvation. With this in mind, let's examine seven things that will most assuredly hinder these three things necessary for one to be saved. I want us to see the seven kinds of people that God will not save.

God Will Not Save the Self-Righteous

In the Gospel of Luke (18:9-14) we look flush into the face of the self-righteous sinner. This is the first kind of person God won't save. "And he spake this parable unto certain which trusted in themselves that they were

26

righteous, and despised others" (v. 9).

I look at people like that every day. I preach to people like this all the time. They trust in themselves. They hardly know anyone quite as wonderful as they are. The way they think of others would be expressed in this way: "My, you're not as righteous as I am. You're not as holy. You're not as wonderful as I am."

In the parable, two men went up to the Temple to pray; the one a Pharisee and the other a publican. "The Pharisee stood and prayed thus with himself, God, I thank thee, that I am not as other men are, extortioners, unjust, adulterers, or even as this publican. I fast twice in the week, I give tithes of all that I possess" (vv. 11-12). Have you ever heard anyone say, "I give tithes of all that I possess."

As the parable continues, "And the publican, standing afar off, would not lift up so much as his eyes unto heaven, but, smote upon his breast saying, God, be merciful to me a sinner" (v. 13). This is when our Lord made his point. Jesus said, "I tell you, this man went down to his house justified rather than the other: for every one that exalteth himself shall be abased; and he that humbleth himself shall be exalted" (v. 14). Jesus said the self-righteous man *went down*. But, the worthless, no-good, filthy sinner, who realized his condition, and bowed his knee and his heart and his life to God was brought into the kingdom of God. Here is one class of people that God will not save: the self-righteous sinner. Those who trust in their works, who trust in their goodness, who trust in their education, who trust in their accomplishments, who trust in their righteousness, who trust in their achievements. They trust in all of those virtues to such a degree that they would be happy to describe the sinner as less than themselves. Jesus said in essence, "This man is not going to get to heaven. The self-righteous will be lost."

America, in past days, had a great revival. Like a prairie fire, it swept across this country. One can still go to places in the world where it is easy to bring about a great Holy Ghost, heaven-sent, powerful revival, with hundreds of people being saved. One can go to India right now and preach, and find hundreds of people streaming down the aisles saying yes to Christ. They will do this in spite of their Hindu background. I know it to be so. What's the difference? The difference is that something happens to a man when you put a good suit on him. Something happens when you surround him with affluence and air conditioning. Something happens to him when you put a pair of alligator shoes on his feet. He becomes a *somebody*.

Jesus said that it would be easier for a camel to go through the eye of a needle than a rich man to be saved. Why? Because when a man is surrounded by all that he himself has accumulated, and earned, and achieved, that man assumes he is pretty good. He's a pretty wonderful man. My dear friend, it's a dangerous thing to live in America because America is "strutting to hell." We've learned how to be cocky and arrogant. This is one kind of man that God won't save!

Let me ask you something. What if we were to go to some affluent area tonight and empty all of the folks from their homes? Suppose we assembled them in one place and preached to those people who belong to effective and very helpful and other civic groups. And suppose we would also preach to the ladies of the hospital auxiliaries where they render so much helpful and sacrificial service. You know, people who are involved in the real *major* issues of life. Imagine preaching to all of those affluent people.

Conversely, what if we were to preach to the folks who are down and out. I'm talking about the drunks who are leaning against brick walls and the fellow who sleeps in his own vomit at night. I'm talking about the man who knows that he's worthless and undone.

On one hand we would preach to the goody-goody, socially involved, wealthy crowd, and on the other hand we would preach to the gutter bums who hang out on skid row. Let me ask you something. From which group of people would we get the better response? You know, and I know. We'd get the better response from skid row bums. I am convinced that when a man stinks of liquor, smells of filth and dirt, he just believes with all of his heart that he's a sinner.

The difficult thing is to convince the achiever and the self-righteous man to see that God doesn't care about how smelly one's clothes are, but rather how is his heart? My friend, we may look good, smell good, drive a good car, or live in a nice home. We may have bank accounts and investments galore. There is nothing wrong with that. The problem is that often we will assume that this is the way in which we get to heaven. How tragic. It would be better to do without things and find salvation than to have the entire world and never make it to heaven. God said for the self-righteous man to be careful. The devil would just as soon send someone to hell in a Hart, Shafner, and Marx suit as overalls. Satan is not proud. He doesn't care. Jesus said the self-righteous will not enter heaven because he won't let himself depend on God. He's righteous in his own mind.

I'm amazed sometimes when I speak to people who think they're educated. I may have three or four more years of education, but, brother, they graduated from some well-known college in some well-known place. They are really the intellectual types, and they vow to be skeptical of the Bible. Listen, my friend, the wisest, most intelligent people on the face of the earth have been believers in the Bible. They have given their hearts and lives to it. Be careful, self-righteous one. Be careful, skeptic. Be careful, those of you who try to find fault. You may find yourself fitting the description of the first kind of person God will not save. *He will not save the self-righteous.*

God Will Not Save Those Who Refuse to Come to Him

The second kind of person God will not save is one who refuses to come unto him for salvation. Look for a moment at John 5:39-40. "Search the scriptures; for in them ye think ye have eternal life: and they are they which testify of me. And ye will not come to me, that ye might have life."

Jesus is making reference to those that search the Scriptures and know that the Scriptures testify of him. They can find him on any page of the Word of God, from Genesis to Malachi; from Matthew to Revelation. However, he goes on to say that they still have not come to him that they might have eternal life. Isn't it interesting how many people want to do everything other than what they ought to do in order to get to heaven? Jesus said there are some with doubts, and sin, and the blindness of Satan who will never allow themselves to come to the Lord. He said they will not have eternal life because they have not come to him.

Some of you have heard me tell about the prodigal son. There is one thing that the father didn't do. Even though he was there with waiting arms, and he was eager to put the shoes on the son's feet, the ring on his

finger, and the robe on his shoulders, there still remained *one thing he didn't do.* He didn't go in the hog
pen to get that boy. Why, I know what a lot of Baptist
churches would have done. They would have gone down
to the hog pen. They wouldn't have waited at the house.
They would have taken out the new member card and
said, "Now, what's your name? Are these your friends? I
see, Oink Jones and Oink Smith here." Two hogs in the
hog pen. But, I want you to know, the father waited
until the son came home.

My friend, there's one thing God will not do. He will
not give anyone salvation unless he comes to Jesus
Christ. God will not do that. God will not cater to our
hang-ups! He'll not scratch the back of our idiosyncrasies. A man will either come the way of the Bible, be
born again by the way of righteousness, which is to come
to Jesus Christ repenting of his sins, or he will not come
at all. There are no shortcuts to heaven. The way of the
cross leads home—the way of repentance—the way of
righteousness. God wants people to realize that they
must come to him in order to be saved. If one does not
come to Jesus, there's no hope for salvation.

Ah! But listen! God has very unusual ways to get
people's attention. Take, for example, the fellow in
church once during a pledge drive. They were asking for
people to volunteer, asking how much money they'd
give. You have heard of this fellow who said, "I'll give
$5.00." About that time a huge glob of plaster fell off the
ceiling and hit the fellow right on the head. He immediately said, "I'll give $500." I'm telling you, if God wants
to convince people, he can. But folks, if God wants to get
people's attention, it may not be so humorous. God has
already done everything necessary to provide for our
pardon. It's not God's move. It's the lost person's move.

God sent his Son. He sent his Holy Spirit. He's tugging and pulling at people's hearts. God has not one obligation to the lost. It's the lost soul's move now. Everything has been done. The stage has been set. God will not save a man who refuses to come to Jesus. If one does not come to Jesus Christ, my friend, there's just no other way for him to be saved. God's not going to make any special case in one's behalf. God will *not* save one who refuses to come to Jesus.

God Will Not Save the Hypocrite

The third kind of person God will not save is found in Matthew 23:13-14. God will not save the hypocrite.

Jesus didn't like some of the Pharisees. I have heard it said, "Preacher, I believe we ought to like everybody." Well, I'm not so sure that is true. "Well," one says, "Jesus had a real love for everyone." Oh, he loved those folks all right.

Notice the passage and its strength. "But woe unto you, scribes and Pharisees, hypocrites! for ye shut up the kingdom of heaven against men: for ye neither go in yourselves, neither suffer ye them that are entering to go in. Woe unto you, scribes and Pharisees and hypocrites! for ye devour widows' houses, and for a pretence make long prayer: therefore ye shall receive the greater damnation." He said two things about these hypocrites. Number 1: they'll never enter the kingdom of God. Number 2: they'll receive a greater hell, a greater judgment, a greater damnation than all of those they talk against.

There are two kinds of hypocrites. One kind of hypocrite is a *church* hypocrite. The other kind is a *nonchurch* hypocrite. The first kind of hypocrite who won't get to heaven is the one who constantly goes to church.

Man, he is there every time the doors are open. He's got a smile on his face from ear to ear. He occasionally drops a token offering into the plate. He may even sing in the choir. He may even teach a class, but deep down in his heart, he's not with it. You know the kind . . . all smiles at church, but at home it's roast the preacher, roast the singer, criticize, criticize, criticize. Oh, he sure hates to miss church because if he did, he wouldn't have anything to gripe about for a whole week. The organ's too loud, or it's too soft. The preacher's too loud, too long, or too short. The singers are too sharp or too flat. I mean everything is just bad. Bad and wrong! My friend, God says that a hypocrite not only shuts the door of heaven, but is in line to a greater damnation and a hotter fire of hell. Why? Well, if one goes to church, and then goes home and gripes and complains, he may not have the Spirit of the living God in him. He may be a scribe, a Pharisee, a hypocrite, who deserves nothing but the very pits of hell. The Lord said it! God cannot save a hypocrite. A hypocrite has shut himself out of the kingdom of heaven and has made hell far worse for himself.

This first kind of hypocrite is a *church* hypocrite. Does this strike home with you, church member? I mean, you go to church, but you're not really with it. You sing in the choir, but not because you love Jesus. You do it because you love music. You come and teach the Bible, but not because you love God. Mainly, it's because you just love to learn. I've often wondered, in my ministry, why some people memorize Scripture and learn the Bible. They could outdo most preachers in a sword drill. But, they have never won anyone to Christ. They've never had the spirit of Job. They've never given sacrificially to the church. I've wondered why.

The reason is probably that the Bible, for them, was

merely another challenge. The Bible for them was merely another venture into scholarship, merely another opportunity to learn. They had a teaching, learning, provocative mind; therefore, the Bible was just like some work of Darwin or Huxley, just like building in their workshop at home. They have known the Book, but they have never known the God of the Book. It is possible to know the Book of the God, and not know the God of the Book. That's the hypocrite who is going to hell. The *church* hypocrite.

The second type of hypocrite is the *nonchurch* hypocrite. He's the kind of person you talk to and say, "Sir, I'd like for you to come to my church sometime and visit with us." He'll say something like this, "God? Do I believe in God? Oh, yes. Oh, yes, I believe in God." By this time he kind of gets a frog in his throat. You ask again, "Do you believe in God?" "Oh, yes," he says, "I believe in God! I believe in God! Yes."

Another phrase that the nonchurch hypocrite uses in answer to the question, "Are you saved?" He says, "Am I saved? Well, I'm probably not saved like you think I ought to be, but I'm saved like I think I ought to be." You've heard that, I'm sure.

The hypocrite who's going to hell may also respond to your question, "My friend, are you saved?" in this way, "Well, I have my own belief. You know, God and I got it going. Yeah! Right! Me and God are so close."

A friend and I were eating in a restaurant the other day, and I witnessed to the waitress. She is a prospect for my wife's Sunday School class. Her father is a former Baptist preacher. I asked, "Do you know Christ as Savior?" The waitress said, "Well, you know, I've got my beliefs." I wonder who ever told her that she had a right to *her own* beliefs? Where does a person get the idea that he can make his own standards?

It is not a matter of believing the way we *want* you to believe. It is a matter of taking God's way. Bailey Smith's way is no better than the way of the dirtiest bum on skid row. We do not have a right to declare, "Yes, I've got my own beliefs about God. I've got my own beliefs about Jesus. I've got my own beliefs about being saved." There's only one way to be saved, and that is to repent of your sins and give your heart and life to Jesus Christ. There is no other way.

Stop trying to edit the Word of God. Quit trying to write your own Bible. You are not qualified! Listen, God says the *nonchurch* hypocrite will never be saved. This kind of hypocrite asserts that he believes in God, but he is never faithful to the things of holiness and righteousness. He wouldn't come to Sunday School! Not on your life! He's too mature for that. He wouldn't come to prayer meeting. Oh, no! He would never give to revival offerings. No! He's got his own beliefs. My friend, the *nonchurch* hypocrite has his belief grounded in the devil himself. The Bible teaches that this kind of hypocrite is eternally lost.

God Will Not Save the Apostate

We come now to the fourth kind of person God will not save. God will not save the apostate.

First of all, I want us to look for a moment at 2 Peter 2:20-22. "For if after they have escaped the pollutions of the world through the knowledge of the Lord and Saviour Jesus Christ, they are again entangled therein, and overcome, the latter end is worse with them than the beginning. For it had been better for them not to have known the way of righteousness, than, after they have known it, to turn away from the holy commandment delivered unto them. But it is happened unto them according to the true proverb, The dog is turned to his own vomit again; and the sow that was washed to her wallowing in the mire."

Do you know what the word *apostate* means? Apostate merely means one who makes a profession of religion and then turns away from it. You say, "Oh, you mean a person can be saved and then lost?" No, that can never happen. I am merely saying that a person who makes a "profession of faith," and is never really saved, is worse off than if he had never made a "profession of faith" to begin with.

Now, with this background, turn to Luke 11:23-25. "He that is not with me is against me: and he that gathereth not with me scattereth. When the unclean spirit is gone out of a man, he walketh through dry places, seeking rest; and finding none, he saith, I will return unto my house whence I came out. And when he cometh, he findeth it swept and garnished." Back up and read in verses 21-22, "When a strong man armed keepeth his palace, his goods are in peace: But when a stronger than he shall come upon him, and overcome him, he taketh from him all his armour wherein he trusted, and divideth his spoils."

My friend, the Bible is teaching that a person may walk the aisle of a church. He may be in tears. He may have people gather all around him to counsel him. It may be an unbelievable, emotional experience. But, if that man does not live a life akin to the life of Christ, he is an apostate. If he makes a profession of belief, but his action does not back it up, God cannot save that kind of man because he is living in the insecure state of never having made a genuine profession of his faith in Christ.

I recently noticed a sign outside another church that

said, "Salvation is not an experience—it's a life."
Brother, that's true. The Bible teaches that if a man
makes a profession of faith and does not live it out, he is
lost. It is better for him not to have made a profession of
faith at all.

When a man makes a false profession of faith, he lives
under the erroneous assumption that he's all right. And
he goes straight to hell thinking that he might one day
go to heaven. What a tragedy! Some who will read this
book have walked down the aisle and have been counseled, but they are apostates. They made a big show of
their profession of faith, and have had a *taste* of religion.
But they are living in the false security of a false experience and a false conversion that is a mere facade. This
person needs to be born again, or he will never see the
inside of heaven. God will not save the apostate.

God Will Not Save Those Who Hold to Unbelief

The fifth kind of person God will not save is the man
who holds to his unbelief. In John 12:39-40 we read,
"Therefore, they could not believe, because that Esaias
said again, He hath blinded their eyes, and hardened
their heart; that they should not see with their eyes, nor
understand with their heart, and be converted, and I
should heal them." There are some that cannot believe.
They hold to their unbelief. They have been blinded.
How were they blinded? Who blinded them? Satan did.
The devil blinded them and they hold to their unbelief.

It is a serious thing to look at the Bible and say, "I
don't know if I believe that." When one does this, he is
calling God a liar. Very few times in my life have I faced
a person and said, "You're lying."

I wrote a letter recently and had to indicate to a well-
known man that he was a liar. I don't do that very often.

It frightens me to call a man a liar. I don't want that said
of me, and I don't like to say it about anyone else. You'd
better think about it before you say to a man, "Buddy,
you're a liar." However, you'd really better make sure
before you say, "God, you're a liar." But for you to put a
question mark on the Bible is for you to call God a liar. A
man who holds to his unbelief and says, "I can't accept
that," is mocking God. Would you call God a liar? God
said that he will not save those who hold to their unbelief. Be careful about calling God a liar.

You know, the Bible says that "Whatsoever a man
soweth, that shall he also reap" (Gal. 6:7). I knew of an
evangelist who went back to his old life and began to do
some things secretly. That indicated he hadn't turned to
God the way he should have. I remember he had his car
fixed one day in Dallas, Texas. At the same time it was
being repaired, he had a brake job. He was driving down
the street right after getting the brakes repaired; they
went out, and he hit another car, head-on. That evangelist is dead. He was a young man, but he is dead.

I believe with all my heart that the evangelist held to
skepticism so long, and doubt about the verities of the
Word, that God had to stop him from preaching in order
that he might not bear a terrible testimony against the
living God. God will not save the man that holds to his
unbelief.

God Will Not Save the Blasphemer

The sixth kind of person that God will not save is a
man that blasphemes the Holy Ghost. Look at Matthew
12:31-32. "Wherefore I say unto you, All manner of sin
and blasphemy shall be forgiven unto men: but the blasphemy against the Holy Ghost shall not be forgiven unto
men. And whosoever speaketh a word against the Son of

man, it shall be forgiven him: but whosoever speaketh against the Holy Ghost, it shall not be forgiven him, neither in this world, neither in the world to come." God will not forgive the man who has blasphemed the Holy Ghost.

You say, "Preacher, how do you blaspheme the Holy Spirit?" There is more than one way to blaspheme the Holy Spirit. For example, I believe some faith healers could have blasphemed the Holy Spirit. If they have, they're lost and God will not forgive them. Lost! To blaspheme the Holy Spirit is to make fun of the Holy Spirit.

I received a brochure through the mail. It stated that if I obtained a particular medallion, I could put it over various parts of my body and the Holy Spirit would heal me. The man who thought of that is in deep spiritual trouble. He is coming close to blaspheming the Holy Spirit. He is making money from little old ladies on Social Security with such ridiculous garbage and nonsense. It repulses me even to think of it.

Recently, I was up late, watching television. I watched a late-night show, and a young lady came on who is a "stripper for Christ." She worked at the Melody Theater in New York City. It just made me shiver when the host said, "We'll be right back after this break to talk to this young lady who is a stripper for the Savior." Do you know what she said in her explanation? She said, "Yes, I dance totally nude for awhile, and the men watching me say they can feel the Holy Spirit on me." Can you believe that? That is what she actually said. Of course, she's wrong, for one thing. You have to be in error to think that way.

Let me tell you something. I felt something sinister come into our room when that lady said what she did. It made me sick to hear her skirt the fringes of blasphemy.

You'd better be careful when you talk about the Holy Spirit making you do something. My friend, it is more than likely *your weird ideas* are making you do it. Don't blame the Holy Spirit for this kind of trash. Be careful. I hear it now, "Oh, Preacher, all of a sudden the Holy Spirit came upon me and I did it. I stripped." Yes, you did it, but the Holy Spirit had nothing to do with it. Be careful.

Let me tell you another way to blaspheme the Holy Spirit. Do you know what may happen as you minister? Some of you are going to have someone tap you on the shoulder or come up to you and say, "I love you in Christ." You may be tempted to say, "That's not God. That's emotionalism. The preacher preached too hard. That music director is singing those tear-jerking songs." My friend, you'd better be careful not to call what's happening "of the world" when it is "of the Holy Spirit."

The Bible says that the work of the Holy Spirit is not to get you to act weird; the work of the Holy Spirit is to convict of sin, and of righteousness, and of judgment. A great Holy Ghost meeting is when a lot of people get saved. When we give the invitation, and something happens to you, and you say, "It's not of God . . . it's not of God," you'd better be careful! You may make a statement that's dreadfully dangerous. Be careful of saying that something is not of the Holy Spirit when it might be. Be careful! The man who blasphemes the Holy Spirit can never be saved.

God Will Not Save Anyone After Death

The seventh kind of person God will not save is a person who has gone out into eternity without Christ. Look in John 8:21, "Then said Jesus again unto them, I go my way, and ye shall seek me, and shall die in your sins: whither I go, ye cannot come."

One who dies in sin can't go with Jesus. It's too late! This person dies without repentance. He dies in cold-heartedness or hardheartedness. He dies in rebellion, and when he stands before the judgment of God, he will protest, "But, Lord, I was good. Lord, I've attended church. Lord, I was active. Lord, I sang in the choir. Lord, I did a lot of good things." But the Lord will say, "Depart from me, I never knew you, you workers of iniquity; and the door of judgment was shut against you, never to be opened again."

Jesus said, "Where I go, you are not going to be able to go." But some may say, "When I stand before my God, I believe he's going to be a God of mercy." Oh, listen! He's a God of mercy, but he's also a God of justice. You will either take him now as a God of mercy, or you will face him later as a God of justice.

You say, "Preacher, you have told us about seven kinds of people that God will *not* save." True! I have. But he will save you if you truly want to be saved. You must be willing to say yes to him, and no to your self-righteousness; no to your unbelief; no to your lack of faith. God is willing to save you. I hope you've not committed the unpardonable sin. I trust that you've not blasphemed the Holy Ghost, and I trust you won't wait until it's too late, because after you are dead there is no hope.

A man said to me, "Preacher, would you pray for my father?" I said, "I sure will. What is his problem?" He replied, "Well, he died." I said, "Why do you want me to pray?" He answered, "Pray that the Lord will take him." I said, "Friend, I can't pray that prayer because I can't pray for anyone who's dead. They are either in heaven or hell."

You say, "Preacher, how do I know whether I have

committed the unpardonable sin?" I believe with all my heart that if you feel the wooing call of the Holy Spirit, or if you feel God's hand upon you, and you desire to respond to this message, you have not committed blasphemy against the Holy Spirit.

My friend, I know that if God speaks to you and you turn him away, you will be as hell-bound as before you began reading this book. You may never in your life have another chance. Be saved now! Now, as you read, receive Jesus as your personal Savior and Lord.

3
Lessons That Lift Life

Several years ago I performed a wedding ceremony for a fellow who said, "Brother Bailey, I'm going to be nervous." I said, "There's no reason to get nervous. Just take a bunch of aspirin right before the ceremony and that will calm you down." I didn't tell him to keep the little metal box in his pocket during the ceremony, but he came out with a big bulge on his leg from that metal box, and all during the ceremony, I heard this, "click, click, click." His knees were not knocking; they were missing one another. I could not believe how frightened he was.

We were repeating the vows, and I reached that part where I said, "And thereto I plight thee my troth." He looked at me and said, "I do what?" He didn't know if he wanted any part of that or not! Through life's experiences, we learn lessons. I learned to always have rehearsals before weddings.

In Jonah 1, we read, "Now the word of the Lord came unto Jonah the son of Amittai, saying, Arise, go to Nineveh, that great city, and cry against it; for their wickedness is come up before me. But Jonah rose up to flee unto Tarshish from the presence of the Lord, and went down to Joppa; and he found a ship going to Tarshish; so he paid the fare thereof, and went down into it, to go with them unto Tarshish from the presence of the Lord. But the Lord sent out a great wind into the sea, and there was a mighty tempest in the sea, so that the ship was like to be broken. Then the mariners were afraid, and cried every man unto his god, and cast forth the wares that were in the ship into the sea, to lighten it of them. But Jonah was gone down into the sides of the ship; and he lay, and was fast asleep" (vv. 1-5). Now, notice verses 15-17, "So they took up Jonah, and cast him forth into the sea: and the sea ceased from her raging. Then the men feared the Lord exceedingly, and offered a sacrifice unto the Lord, and made vows. Now the Lord had prepared a great fish to swallow up Jonah. And Jonah was in the belly of the fish three days and three nights." Notice chapter 2, verse 10, "And the Lord spake unto the fish, and it vomited out Jonah upon the dry land."

God Is Inescapable

One of the lessons that stands out so undeniably in this book is that *God is inescapable.* The word of the Lord came to Jonah, and the Bible declares that God wanted Jonah to go to Nineveh. Instead of going to Nineveh, Jonah turned his back upon the voice of God and went exactly opposite to what God said. Instead, he went to Tarshish.

Jonah thought that just because he got on a ship, he could escape God. God had said to go one way, and Jonah was going another way. Jonah assumed that God could be lost in all of Jonah's disobedience. Jonah should have known better. He should have known that God is inescapable. Think of the extreme measures that God took in proving that to Jonah. Imagine a man being swallowed by a fish! What an unbelievable, ridiculous thing—it seems to modern science—to think that such could happen. But God wanted to let us know that we cannot get away from him. He will even use a fish, or something worse, to swallow us.

He can use a circumstance, a tragedy, or a difficulty in life to swallow us—to let us know we cannot escape God. The Bible states that the fish swallowed Jonah, came over to the side, and vomited Jonah out upon dry land. We know the sea isn't dry, and the land near the sea isn't dry because that's where the waves come to and fro and make this land damp and wet.

Is the Bible wrong to say that the fish spit Jonah upon dry land? No, because we know what the Bible is pointing out. It is saying that the fish didn't come up and just casually spit Jonah out. Jonah made that fish sick at its stomach. Like being shot from a cannon, Jonah went way in where the land was bone-dry. I believe this account is in the Bible to show that God did not want Jonah to be so near the water that the waves of disobedience and rebellion would catch him and take him back out into the sea of unconcern. God is inescapable!

Rome should have learned that as a nation. We cannot get away from God. There was a day in the Roman Empire when the people thought they could escape from God. They said, "No, we don't need God." Professional begging was legalized during the reign of the Roman Empire. The professional beggars would go around to peasants and steal their infants. They'd take those little babies and break their arms and legs, and those infants would grow up with broken bodies. They would grow in grotesque, horrible fashion, and, as the children got older, they would be deposited around the city of Rome with tin cups in their hands because they made great, pitiful beggars. That's the way the beggars made their living. During the time of the Roman Empire, people said; "We don't need God. God, get lost." But God brought Rome to its knees.

Germany thought the same. Germany thought, *We don't need God. We are an Aryan race. We had the U-2 rocket before Americans ever thought of rockets. We know how to take oxygen and make liquid out of it. We are brilliant.* They killed millions and millions of people. Germany said, "We don't need God." Hitler killed those great preachers who proclaimed the undeniable truths of God, but there came a day when God said, "Germany, you've had it," and Germany learned it couldn't get away from God.

America needs to know, as a nation, that we must straighten up, clean up our lives, get rid of immorality, and come back to God, or America will feel the wrath of the hand of God. God is inescapable. Every nation must learn that.

People who are lost must also learn that. A man may turn down an evangelistic invitation. He may reject the work of the Holy Spirit, live to be one hundred years of age, and say, "Man, I've gotten away from God. I've turned down invitations, my wife's tried to get me to go to revivals, but no one ever got me down an aisle. I've never been saved. I've never turned on to God, and I have escaped God. I'm not going to respond to that invitation." But the Bible says, "After this the judgment" (Heb. 9:27). God has the last word about us. We may deny God for as long as we live, but after this life we will stand face to face and answer for what we did. God is inescapable.

But it's also true for the people on whom he has placed his hand. After I was called to preach, I went to Fort Worth to visit a relative who said, "Bailey, I'm so glad that you've given your life to preach. God called me to preach." I said, "Uncle Frank, I never knew you preached." He said, "Oh, I've never preached, but God called me to preach. You know, when I was a seventeen-year-old boy the voice of God came to me and told me to preach, but I denied him. We operate this washateria next door, and when I am there, those old wringer machines seem to say, as they work, 'Frank, you should have preached. You should have preached.' I go to bed at night, turn off the light, and in that darkness there seems to be a ghostly, ghastly voice that says over and over, 'Frank, you should have preached. You should have preached.' "

If God ever puts his hand upon a man to preach, direct music, be an educational director, a youth director, or a missionary, God will never take that hand of calling from him. A person may not do it, but he'll always know that he has been called. We cannot get away from God. We may not do what he asks, but we will always live in the horrible abyss of realizing we have missed life's best.

Our Sins Affect Other People

God is inescapable, but we need to remember that our sins affect other people. Jonah was on board the ship and everyone was scared to death. Who was disobedient? Only one. The Bible says those big, strong mariners were scared to death. The sea became tempestuous, the ship rocked to and fro, and everyone was discouraged because of one man's sin. Jonah should have been in Nineveh, preaching, winning souls, saving lives, and making homes go back together, but the people of Nineveh were suffering. They were suffering because one rebellious prophet was out in a ship somewhere, or in the belly of a fish, trying to get his life right. Our sins affect other people.

Sometime ago I preached on the prodigal son. What a glorious victory it was when the prodigal son came home, received the ring on his finger, sandals on his feet, and the robe wrapped around his shoulders. But I wonder about that man in the foreign land from whom the prodigal may have stolen, about those who saw him eating husks in the hog pen, and about the girls with whom he may have committed fornication. I wonder if they ever knew that he finally got right? The prodigal son may have condemned their souls to hell while he came home and ate the fatted calf.

Man can stop sinning, but he cannot stop the consequences of his sin. A man discovered that his little girl was having problems with her eyes. He carried her to a doctor in Dallas who felt the problems needed the services of a specialist in Chicago. They went to Chicago and, after the examination, the specialist asked the father if he could be examined, also. The father said, "I'm not sick."

"I know," said the doctor, "but we need to examine you."

Although he did not understand why, the father agreed to have the examination. Afterwards, the doctor called the father into the inner office and said, "Sir, what we suspected is true. Let me ask you something. Were you ever immoral, promiscuous, or did you ever take any liberties before you were married?"

He said, "Well, yes, I have to admit I did while I was in the service."

The doctor said, "We have discovered that you have a disease in your body which you have passed into the life of your little girl. Your little girl has your disease, and because of it, she is going to lose her sight."

That man looked at the doctor and said, "Doctor, are you telling me that because of what I did ten or twelve years ago, my little girl is going to be blind?"

The doctor said, "That's right. I'm afraid your little girl is going to go blind."

That man came back and joined a church in East Dallas. He got right with God, and got so concerned that he became a deacon in the church.

Now he wins souls and gives his money to God. God has forgiven him, and that slate is wiped absolutely clean. His sins have been forgiven and they have been cast as far as the east is from the west. But, in spite of everything that man has done for God, his little girl will live in darkness all of the days of her life. A man can get right with God and straighten up his life, but seeds that he has planted will bring a harvest he will never be able to stop. One can stop his sinning, but he can't stop the consequences of sin.

I talked with a man in Lovington, New Mexico, one time who bragged about being lost. He had five boys, and every one of them bragged about being lost, just like their father. They were all apparently headed for hell. What a horrible thing it is for a father's rejection of God to influence a son, a daughter, a neighbor, or a friend. No one goes to hell alone—he always takes someone else with him. Our sins affect other people.

A lady was shaking her daughter, saying, "You kids of this generation. You've got all this long hair and loud music. You don't pay attention to your parents like I did when I was growing up. Why, when I was growing up, I wasn't like you. I wasn't rebellious like you. I didn't like all these fads that you do. You teenage girls and boys are not like we were when we were growing up." The daughter said, "Mom, maybe you had better parents than we do."

A man came to me one time in a church where I was pastor and said, "Preacher, you know, for a long time I didn't get saved. But now I'm turned on to God. I really love Jesus." I said, "Yes sir, I know it." He continued, "I went to a neighboring town and witnessed to my son. I told him that all of his life I was out of the will of God. I was wrong. I was rebellious against God. As I tried to witness to him, he looked at me and said, 'Daddy, you made me what I am. Now, leave me alone.' "

That man looked at me, and tears came pouring down his cheeks. With a broken voice he cried, "Preacher, I'm living in a saved man's hell." "A saved man's hell" is a hell created by a man saved too late to save anyone but himself.

Some think about getting right with God, think about being saved, think about really turning their lives over to Jesus, but in the meantime, they can scar, maim, or cripple the lives of those they know and love. No matter how saintly we turn someday, it will be too late to undo what we have already done. Jonah had to learn that our sins always affect other people.

God's Will Is Life's Greatest Joy

Thirdly, God's will is life's greatest joy. God said, "Jonah, go to Nineveh." "No, God, I want to go to Tarshish," replied Jonah. I can imagine that Jonah began to rationalize, "Now, God, there are people in Nineveh, but there are also people in Tarshish. There are lost people in Nineveh, but there are also lost people in Tarshish, too." God didn't tell Jonah to go where logic seemed to direct him. God told him, "Go to Nineveh." The greatest thing in the world is to know that we are in the will of God. I'd rather be in the will of God than to be worth 500 million dollars, or be some kind of famous celebrity.

Sometimes young people come to me crying, "I just

don't know what I'm going to do. I know God wants me to go to school, but I don't know if I have the money or not."

When I went off to college I had $450, and I just knew that was going to carry me through school. In two days I was absolutely broke. I needed some money. I had to get myself through school, but my parents didn't have any money to send me. An invitation came to Ouachita Baptist University for someone to be a youth director, so I was sent to the First Baptist Church of Brinkley, Arkansas. I went up on a Saturday night, stayed in a hotel, and went to services the next Sunday morning. They told me that I was going to be the youth director with the weekly salary of $35! In those days, for that kind of money I would have been lifeguard for the baptistry! I'd never heard of a youth director. I didn't know what youth directors did. The little church where I grew up didn't have anyone on the staff. I didn't know what a "staff" was. At my home church, my father was the preacher, but he didn't have a staff.

That Sunday morning the pastor of the church handed me *The Broadman Hymnal* and said, "Now, Bailey, just pick out any songs that you want to lead us in today." I asked, "Is that what youth directors do?" He said, "That job is music/youth director." I said, "Man, I can't sing." He said, "You're going to sing." I got up on Sunday morning and began leading the singing.

That Sunday afternoon, I met with their committee, and, of all the silly things, that committee called me to be their music/youth director. I couldn't believe it! I couldn't even sing!

Monday I went into one of those old Arkansas stores that has striped mattresses, oval bathtubs, and horse collars hanging around, and bought a suit for $7.50.

Going back my old car broke down, and I had to buy a new generator. That cost me $18. I got back to school, but I was so frustrated for spending some of the money that I had gotten.

Then I made my next mistake. I decided to wear that new suit to a football game, and it rained, as it can only rain in Arkansas, on my expensive $7.50 suit. I sent the suit to the cleaners, and when I brought it back down the hall, the fellows said, "Hey, have you got your little brother's suit?" You can't believe how it had shrunk. I was the only boy in Arkansas with Bermuda shorts with a coat to match!

I picked up the phone and called the pastor of that church. I said, "Brother McCoy, I ain't coming. The Lord didn't want me to be a youth director. He wanted me to be a preacher." In just one month, at the age of nineteen, I was pastor of a church, and I've been a pastor of a Southern Baptist church ever since. God didn't want me to be a music director, and he didn't want me to be a youth director. He wanted me to be a preacher. When I learned that, it was a comfortable feeling.

Some people are so worried because they think everything is going to be bad if they line up with the will of God. I remember dating and wanting to have a nice wife who loved me. At that time I was going with a girl who had already been voted a beauty in college. I prayed to God and said, "Lord, I just know that's the girl I ought to marry." She was a gorgeous girl, and I just knew that she was the woman God wanted me to marry. But the Lord said, "No." I said, "Lord, look a little bit closer. I know this is the one I ought to marry." But the Lord refused to let that girl be the one, and now I see why. I could never improve on the wife God gave me.

If God shuts any door, we can trust in him perfectly,

and things will be much better than we could ever imagine. The will of God is the world's greatest joy. Jonah should have known that, too.

God Will Not Hesitate to Send a Storm

The last lesson is that God will not hesitate to send a storm to get you where you ought to be. Why did Jonah turn back to God? Because of the storm. Had it not been for that storm on the ship, the men on board would not have cast Jonah overboard. Had they not cast Jonah overboard, a fish would never have swallowed him to get him back where God wanted him.

Some dear people are active members of the First Baptist Church of Hobbs, New Mexico. They never entered that church while I was pastor there, except approximately once a year. But there came a time when I went out to a grave site and stood over a tiny casket. This good man and his wife had just lost their little baby. I led the wife to know the Lord, and she was baptized. He became active in our church. The last year I was there, they were there on Sunday morning and Sunday night, dedicated to the Lord. Did the Lord take that little baby? I don't know, but I have a suspicion that its death was not necessarily the intentional will of God. I also know that it's horrible when tragedy must come before a person will awaken to be where God wants him to be. Remember, God is inescapable. Your sins *will* affect other people. God's will is life's greatest joy. God will not hesitate to send a storm into your life to place you where he wants you.

4
Being Good Is Not Enough

Some time ago a book told of our young men in Korea under the awful brainwashing of the North Korean Communists. It described how many men were not able to be loyal to their country and have courage in the midst of the horrible interrogation of the Communists. Many of our young soldiers cursed their country, said they hated their mothers, and spit upon the American flag.

It would be easy for me to stand, surrounded by friends, in a comfortable building, and say, "I would never do that." I might even boast of more courage, patriotism, and intestinal fortitude than they demonstrated. But we must beware before we criticize. We first need to know the position of someone else. The old Indian saying is right, "Don't talk about how another brother walks until you have walked a mile in his moccasins."

Those soldiers were perhaps good men, but there is a time in which being good is not enough. Being good is not adequate. Being good is to admit defeat. Being good is insufficient.

One Sunday morning a young, brokenhearted husband came down the aisle of our church. He refused to talk to one of our associates, but he motioned to me. I knelt with him, and he put his face near my ear and said, "Pastor, I was out of town last weekend and the charms of a promiscuous woman were so great that I could not resist, and I was immoral. My heart is broken. I don't know if God can ever forgive me."

That man was a good man and is a good man. He believes the Bible. He's trusted in Christ, and his life has given testimony of what it is to be right with God. But he made a horrible mistake. He's a good man, but being good is not good enough. Being good is not always adequate or sufficient.

In a Texas city is a church that has an auditorium with a seating capacity of over 2,000 people. It is located on a very busy thoroughfare, and if one were to go there today, he would find Bible-believing, good people. And yet, in an auditorium that seats more than 2,000, there will be less than 300 people on a given Sunday . . . Bible-believing people . . . good people . . . moral people . . . people of character and integrity and honesty . . . good people . . . but good is not enough. Without a deeper walk with God, a deeper commitment to God, a new experience and touch from God, and a new fire from heaven, a man is headed toward destruction, failure, compromise, and embarrassment. Being good is not enough.

Look at Daniel 6:4-5, "Then the presidents and princes sought to find occasion against Daniel concerning the kingdom; but they could find none occasion nor fault; forasmuch as he was faithful, neither was there any error or fault found in him. Then said these men, We shall not find any occasion against this Daniel, except we find it against him concerning the law of his God."

Had Daniel been only a good man, he would never have been able to withstand the pressures that he faced. But Daniel was a man that had a certain walk with God. I don't know about you, but I would like to be like P. P. Bliss's song says,

Dare to be a Daniel,
Dare to stand alone,
Dare to have a purpose firm!
Dare to make it known!

PHILIP P. BLISS

Daniel was a good man, but he was more than that. The name Daniel means "God is judge." When one looks at Daniel's life, he finds untold numbers of people who were judged by the unbelievably high standard of the life of Daniel. What a man he was! From the time he was a boy until the experience in the den of lions, God called Daniel the "beloved" (Dan. 9:23; 10:11).

Here was a man who was the prime minister of the Medo-Persian Empire, the most powerful nation on earth. Daniel was the prime minister. Don't believe that for a man to be godly he must be a failure or be poor or that he must be down and out and not able to make it in life! Any job that needs to be done can be done by a Spirit-filled child of God. Daniel was a man who had risen to the second place in the whole Persian empire, second only to King Darius. Daniel was a man who endured some things because he was more than just a good man.

We live in a generation in which we are going to face critical times of life. It's going to take more than being good women, good men, good teenagers, and good college students to be successful in our world because the world is going to test us for every ounce of spiritual fiber we have.

Dedication to the Will of God

The dedication of Daniel speaks in at least three different avenues of expression. Here is a man who had a deep dedication to the will of God. Daniel 6:23 says,

"Then was the king exceeding glad for him and commanded that they should take Daniel up out of the den. So Daniel was taken up out of the den, and no manner of hurt was found upon him, because he believed in his God." God not only wants men in heaven, he wants heaven in men.

A few years ago Arkansas football coach Lou Holtz was interviewed and asked, "Coach Holtz, is it true that your life's ambition, ever since you were a boy, has been to be the coach of Ohio State." Holtz replied, "Yes, that's right." The interviewer said, "You've always thought it a great step forward to follow Woody Hayes?" Holtz again said, "Yes." The interviewer then said, "I understand that they've telephoned you about coming to be the coach at Ohio and have offered you the job!" Holtz replied, "Yes, they have, but I'm not going." "But it's your life's ambition," said the sportscaster. "You've always wanted to do it. You've got the opportunity. Why aren't you going?" I'll never forget his answer. Holtz said, "Because I have a commitment to Arkansas." Just a matter-of-fact, blanket, unqualified, unvarnished, unmitigated commitment.

It really doesn't matter what advantageous opportunities we have along the way. Nothing should be in our lives that would interfere with the fact that one day the Holy Spirit of God spoke to our hearts and said to each of us, "I want you to be my child." He came in and saved us by the power of God. As of that day, hell was a closed option. It doesn't matter what opportunities come our way. We have made a commitment to God. It's settled!

But sometimes we lose the burning zeal we once had for God. Cliff Barrows told me that Billy Graham once walked into his staff meeting and told all of his staff, "I want you to know that the evangelist, Billy Graham, needs a new walk with God." Every now and then we just need a new touch.

Dedication to the Way of God

Secondly, we need a new dedication to the *way* of God. It is possible to do *what* God wants us to do, but not the *way* God wants us to do it. As a pastor, I must desire not only to accomplish what he wants in winning souls and building up the saints and growing an evangelistic church, but also to do it the *way* he wants me to do it. I don't want to just do it in an expedient way, or a political way—I want to do it God's way!

We also must have a new dedication to the Word of God. I remember as a little child we used to sing the chorus, "The B-I-B-L-E."

> The B-I-B-L-E
> Yes, that's the book for me;
> I stand alone on the Word of God:
> The B-I-B-L-E.

We must stand on God's Word.

Most Christians don't spend enough time in the Bible. The Bible can be read leisurely in eighty hours. If one will just take fifteen minutes a day, one can read the Bible in a year, and God will give you ten hours back.

One thing I notice about Daniel—he believed what God said. Don't say, "I can't do it. I can't be what so-and-so is. I can't be that kind of Christian." You can be the kind of Christian you are willing to let God make you. In reality, you are the kind of Christian you want to be.

I've heard people say, "I'd like to be like some of these great Spirit-filled men in our church." But these men of God didn't get that way by only desiring to be; they got that way by submitting themselves to the power, presence, and the availability of God. That's the only way. We must pray that God will touch our souls and burn within us a new dedication to God.

Not only must we have a new *dedication,* we must also have a new *discipline.* I don't know anyone quite so disciplined as was Daniel. We need a new discipline in three areas of life.

We need a new discipline in our personal lives. I long to have the kind of life so honoring to God that one could interview my wife very closely, and she would have nothing bad to say about me. I don't want my own children to see me living at home in such a way that would adversely affect what they think of a preacher. Many sons of preachers have gone bad. Maybe it's because they didn't see the daddy at home that they saw in the pulpit.

We should desire a new discipline for our lives so that even in the weakest moment, the most frail moment of our lives, we will not bring a black eye to the reputation of God. Daniel was consistent even in the privacy of his home. When Daniel knew that the edict restricting prayer had been signed, he went into his house, and with the windows in his chamber open toward Jerusalem, he kneeled three times a day, prayed, and gave thanks before his God. If we'd just burst open the average Christian's home, I wonder what we would see? If we had a movie of the average marriage last week, how would it look? It would be kind of sad, wouldn't it?

If someone could delve into the darkest chambers of our minds and reveal the contents to everyone, what would be seen? We need a new discipline in our personal lives to be the kind of people that God wants us to be even in the most intimate, private moments.

But, we also need a *new discipline in our prayer lives.*
We should love to get with God in prayer! A man in Florida once told me, "You know, one of the secrets of First
Southern Baptist Church in Del City is the prayer life of
Jake Self." That's true. Jake bugs me all the time. I can't
even talk to him because he always wants to pray. I can
say, "Brother Jake, I want to talk to you about something," and he will say, "Don't talk—let's pray." It's just
impossible to talk to him. He wants to pray! He prays
about praying! It's good to know that there is a man on
the church staff who believes that it is better to talk to
God about men than to talk to men about other men.

We've got to pray. It's amazing, in fact, almost shock-
ing, but God always has a better answer than I do. At
times, I don't see how God makes it without my wisdom,
but he does!

Many times we say that we believe in prayer, but we
don't. I remember years ago, in the West Texas area of
Midland and Odessa, it became extremely dry. A little
church out there, where the mesquite bushes and
tumbleweeds were blowing across the dry, dusty roads,
got together and had a great prayer meeting for rain. As
they began to pray, unbelievably, a great black cloud
hovered over that little church and the rains came in
torrents during the prayer meeting. The people came to
the front door and said, "How in the world are we going
to get to our cars without getting wet?" A little twelve-
year-old girl came through the crowd and said, "Well, I
brought my umbrella since we were praying for rain. Do
you want to borrow it?" We ought to have such power
with God, and such freedom in praying that when we
pray for rain, we bring an umbrella.

We should get ready for God to work. We ought to
pray for souls to be saved, and then we ought to get out

in the aisles and watch them come. That kind of prayer opens the windows of heaven and the fire of God falls when we pray like that.

We need a new discipline in our personal lives, in our prayer lives, and even *in our public lives.*

You can tell a lot about a person by observing how public he is about his faith. Occasionally I go into a business owned by a church member, and I find a picture of Christ on the wall. Some may think that will offend others. Sometimes I go to the office of one of our professional men, the lawyers or doctors, and there among his books I will find the Word of God. I become excited about that.

I tried to encourage a man to be a bold witness one day, and he said to me, "Well, Preacher, I just have the conviction that religion is a very personal matter." Listen, it is a very personal matter, but when you have Jesus, it's going to be a public matter, too. Jesus does not lead anyone to join "Christians Anonymous." He wants no "Lone-Ranger" Christians. He wants no secret disciples. A man with Christ in his heart can no more hide that than one can hide the fragrance of a rose under a hairnet. If Jesus is in a man's life, it is somehow going to be exposed. We shouldn't be obnoxious, cantankerous, or uncooperative. But one cannot have the sweet spirit of Christ radiating in one's life and keep it down.

If all I had was religion, I wouldn't tell anyone, anyway. It ought to be kept very personal. In fact, it ought to be buried. But Jesus gets rid of the religion and gives man a way of life. Marriage is very private and personal, but I want you to know I love Sandy Smith. I'm not ashamed of her. Marriage is personal, but I tell everybody I love my wife. I'd die for her; and I want you to know I love Jesus, and I'd die for him.

Dedication to the Word of God

Thirdly, we need a new daring in faith. Daniel dared. They said, "Daniel, don't pray." And the Bible says as soon as he heard what they had said, he prayed. God gave him courage and fortitude to pray.

We need three kinds of daring faith. We need a faith that *attempts*. We need to attempt some great things for God. We may fail, but so what? All I am anyway is a failure.

Simon Peter has often been criticized for his actions the night Jesus walked on water. Jesus told Peter to walk with him. He got out, walked on the water, and then fell into the water. But, it's better to sink in the water *with* Jesus than to be in the boat *without* him. At least Simon Peter is the only man, outside of Jesus, who has taken one step on water! Here was a man who had faith enough to attempt.

Great preachers are often criticized for ideas. Some have some wild, imaginative, creative plans, and many may have made some blunders, but while they were making blunders, they were doing something for God. I appreciate a man who is just "stupid" enough to go forward for God.

What shame unto God if we build walls around ourselves and say, "God, you've done good enough. We've got the biggest church in our town or state. We've done enough."

I was with Jerry Falwell at a James Robison Bible Conference in 1979. I was talking to Dr. Falwell about his church budget and asked him how much it took for them to operate. He said, "Well, we're bringing in about $1 million a week." I said, "What? A million a week!" At that time our church operated on $2 million a year, and we thought we were wonderful. But $52 million a year is no money to God.

How big is our God? He is sometimes pretty small according to the way we think. We need not be worried about failure—just about missing his will. We must have the faith that attempts great things for God.

We also need faith that *accepts*. When we step out for God, we've got to accept some things. Daniel stepped out for God, and he was put in a den of lions. Had Daniel merely been a good man, he would have been a failure. When the testing of greatness comes, if we're only good, we'll fail. But, if we're of God, we'll do something. That's the difference.

One thing we must accept is the judgment of the world. The world looked at Daniel and despised him. The Bible says, in Daniel 6:4, that no one could find "occasion nor fault; forasmuch as he was faithful, neither was there any error or fault found in him." Then they said, "Let's get him."

The more successful we become as children of God, the more angry the world will get. But we need to love our critics. Even when we're in the will of God, one of the things we've got to accept is criticism. It's going to come.

Not only do we need to accept the trouble that is going to come, but we need to accept the fact that God is able. Daniel went into that den of lions knowing God was able. What a man of faith he was! One thing that has always bothered me about the story of Daniel and the den of lions was the fact that even though the Bible says an angel came and shut the mouths of the lions, the Bible never said anything about those long claws. Have you ever seen a lion's claws? They're long! I wonder what Daniel thought when he saw the angel come and close the mouths of the lions? The angel just went over there and put a zipper on their mouths. But Daniel looked over there and saw those long claws. Sometimes those lions would stretch and extend those claws. You wouldn't have to be eaten to death. You could be *clawed* to death!

I think God shut the mouth of the lions, but left the claws because as I've learned about the will and the purpose of God, God gives us just enough safety to keep us on our knees. Had Daniel seen those lions as absolutely incapable of harming him, he might have said, "Ha! Ha! Good old comfortable Daniel. I don't have one problem in the world." But every time he looked at the shut mouths, he'd see those claws and say, "God, I still need you. God, I still need you." God wants us to be dependent upon him.

When Daniel was put in the den of lions, he didn't say, "No, don't do that." Neither did Daniel get on his knees and pray, "Oh, God, don't let them put me in the den of lions," because he knew he was going to the den of lions. If the only time we pray is when a crisis comes, we just may not get through. Daniel didn't need to pray just because he was thrown in the den of lions because prayer was part and parcel of his life. Every particle of Daniel was a particle that communed with a holy God. Therefore, when a crisis came, he just talked with God the same as he always did. Some people wait until a funeral, car wreck, or a bad report from the surgeon to pray. Prayer should be so familiar with us that we've got God's attention all the time.

Last of all, we need to see a new *demonstration* of the power of God. Daniel came to a time of safety in the den of lions because of the demonstration of God's power. Daniel 6:27 says, "He delivereth and rescueth, and he worketh signs and wonders in heaven and in earth, who hath delivered Daniel from the power of the lions."

When God's will is done and God's work is done and God's way is done, Jesus is glorified. The Bible says that the King of kings was honored. Not old Darius, but the King of kings.

There's quite a contrast between Darius in the palace and Daniel in the den. Daniel was asleep and at peace. He may have told the lions to move over. He may have said, "Come here, pussycat. I want to put my head on you for a pillow." The king was in the palace with war in his soul. Daniel was in the den of lions and had the safety of God, but the king was back home not knowing who was about to topple him from his throne. It is better to be in a den of lions *with* God than to be in a palace *without* God. Safety is not the absence of danger, but rather the presence of God.

In 1 Peter 3:10-13 the Bible says, "For he that will love life, and see good days, let him refrain his tongue from evil, and his lips that they speak no guile: Let him eschew evil, and do good; let him seek peace, and ensue it. For the eyes of the Lord are over the righteous, and his ears are open unto their prayers: but the face of the Lord is against them that do evil. And who is he that will harm you, if ye be followers of that which is good?" We have nothing to fear when our King is honored. We need to see a new demonstration of the power of God.

5
A Babbling Preacher
and a Strange Gospel

If you were to travel at the speed of light (more than 186,000 miles per second), in two seconds you would be past the moon; in eight minutes, you would be past the sun; in four months, you would be at the edge of our solar system; and in five years, you would be to the nearest star, Alpha Centauri A. If you were to travel 100,000 years at that incredible speed, you would finally exit from our galaxy, better known as the Milky Way. If you decided to go to the next closest galaxy, called the Great Nebuli, you would travel for 1,500,000 years at the speed of 186,000 miles per second to get there.

Scientists now have telescopes that can see four and one-half billion light-years into space. And yet the Bible says that our God holds all of that in the palm of his hand. He must be a mighty and powerful God. Everyone ought to fall in love with a God like that, but they don't. A person that doesn't serve God in light of his power ought to appear stupid and idiotic.

We live in a world that has rejected the great and mighty God. But why? According to the Bible, it's because the heart of man is wicked and he is filled with sin. Jeremiah 17:9 says, "The heart is deceitful above all things and desperately wicked." Not just mildly wicked, but *desperately* wicked, and "all our righteousnesses are as filthy rags" (Isa. 64:6).

Instead of living in a world that is conducive to the preaching of God and his Son, Jesus Christ, we live in a world that counts the gospel of Christ as strange and foreign.

Years ago a man by the name of Paul preached, and when he finished preaching, they dubbed him a "babbler" and called his message "strange" (Acts 17:8). For these philosophers to call Paul strange would be like the Ayatollah Khomeini calling Billy Graham weird. They did so because they could not understand the gospel of Jesus Christ.

What made them call Paul a babbler and his gospel a "strange" gospel? When we see what he preached, we can understand why the finger of accusation was pointed at Paul. We can then understand why those who heard Paul said the gospel of Christ was strange.

Read through the entire chapter of Acts 17 and you will find many references to the fact that Paul was mocked and scoffed at. In essence, Paul was told, "We'll hear you again later. Don't call us, we'll call you."

Commitment Is More Than Curiosity

Anyone that preaches the unadulterated, unmitigated, untarnished truth of God preaches at least four things the modern world thinks to be strange. First, Paul preached that commitment is more necessary than curiosity. If you wonder where that comes from, look in Acts 17:21. The Bible says the Athenians and strangers which were in Athens spent their entire time either telling or hearing some "new" thing. (A lot of present-day churches major in nothing else!) These Athenians were intellectually curious, and loved every new thought like a hummingbird trying to taste the nectar of every flower in the garden. These philosophers flitted from one academic blossom to another. New thoughts, new ideas, and little tidbits helped the Athenian philosophers learn to doubt the Bible.

Those who seek to explain that miracles aren't true, that there isn't a second coming, and that there is reason to doubt the Word of God need to be avoided! Don't listen to a hell-bound professor tell you he's curious about some "new idea" that conflicts with the Word of God.

The message of the apostle Paul was not a message of curiosity *about* the Word of God, it was commitment *to* the Word of God. Paul looked at the Athenians and said, "Ye men of Athens . . . ye are too superstitious [or religious]" (Acts 17:22). Actually, that's what the word *superstitious* means. America's problem is "being too religious." Instead of having religion that stamps "hell" upon our lives and eternity, we need Jesus Christ who sets us free. Jesus Christ is not one of many choices you have regarding a religious experience. Anyone can have a religious experience, but what man needs is a complete commitment of life to Christ.

I knew a preacher of another denomination who always told me about new, curious ideas he'd heard. He would often ask, "Who are you reading?" He always wanted to know what books I was currently reading or what authors I had followed. I enjoyed teasing him by saying, "Man, I've found a new author—he's Matthew," or, "It's Mark," or, "It's Daniel," or, "It's Ezekiel." He never liked that. He'd tell me he was reading "Dr. Bad Breath" or "Professor Fuzzy Fact" or some philosopher I had never heard of. He would often go off to some liberal university to study and come back with more doubts and more inconsistencies than he already had. He would give dry garbage to his people instead of spiritually feeding them. These people were spiritually hungry and starved! Once he said, "I want you to go with me to a school in the East. We've got a new allegorical interpretation of Genesis 1:3."

I'm not curious about Genesis. I'm committed to it! I'm not curious about the virgin birth of Christ. I'm committed to it! I'm not curious about the bodily resurrection. I'm committed to it! I'm not curious about the great return of the Lord Jesus Christ. I'm committed to it! I'm not curious whether this Bible is the infallible, inerrant Word of God. I'm committed to it! Yet, we have produced a generation of people who are interested in nothing else but to tell or to hear some "new thing."

There was a cello player who kept his hand in one place while all the other cello players went up and down the strings. Someone said, "Why don't you move your hands up and down like all the cello players?" He said, "They're looking for it, and I've found it."

You don't need to move away from Jesus Christ. I'm not a fanatic, I'm just saved! This is not the time to be curious about the wild, the weird, the way-out, but it is high time to be committed to the great, sane, saving, sensible, old-time, all-the-time, new-time, now-time, anytime, glorious gospel of Jesus Christ. Don't get curious—get committed!

Curiosity not only killed the cat, it is about to bury your neighbor. Unless we quit trying new religions, new drinks, new entertainment, new freedom, new perversions, America is doomed. America needs to get rid of its curiosity and get back to the basic truths of the Word of God. There is no hope apart from the truth of God's Word.

A scientist went to Arkansas to fish and hired a guide that he thought wasn't very smart for his canoe. This scientist was a pseudointellectual and he said to his guide as they were traveling along, "Have you ever measured the viscosity of this water? The guide said,

"Nope." The man saw some pretty flowers, and asked, "Have you ever studied botany?" "Nope," was the reply. "You've missed half of your life," said the scientist, and then asked, "Have you ever studied chemistry?" The guide answered, "Nope, I know a lot about cornbread, but not chemistry." Again, the scientist said, "You've missed half of your life." He looked at the sky and said, "Have you ever studied astronomy?" The guide simply answered, "Nope." The scientist said, "Man, you've missed half of your life!" About that time the canoe turned over. The guide was swimming to shore and the scientist was going down for the second time when the guide hollered, "Do you know how to swim?" The scientist screamed, "No!" The guide replied, "You've missed *all* your life." Nothing is going to keep this country afloat apart from commitment to Christ.

Religion Is Not Separated from Righteousness

Not only was Paul's gospel strange because it had more commitment than curiosity, but, secondly, Paul believed that religion was never separated from righteousness.

The people of Paul's day believed they could have a religion that would not affect their lives. This is why they called Paul a babbler. Those with whom Paul talked separated religion from life.

The Pharisees mocked him because their religion was really an external affair. That's why Jesus had called them whited sepulchers—white on the outside, but like tombs on the inside.

The Stoics who believed in a metaphysical approach to life and the Epicureans were, in reality, atheists. As you look at each of the philosophical schools, you see their idea was religion as a study, a plaything, or something simply to talk about.

I have found while visiting that people have an interest in religion. But Jesus Christ is not going to allow anyone the luxury of adopting him as part of a hobby in life. Jesus Christ doesn't want to be a thread in the garment of a person's life. He wants to be the pattern from which the whole garment is made. Everything!

There is a publisher of a porno magazine who says he has been born again. If he has been born again, he no doubt would have ceased publishing that magazine. There is no question about it. When a man has been changed, he'll not publish filth.

The Bible never tells us not to judge, but it says not to judge unless we are willing to be judged on the same basis. If I am caught publishing a magazine like that, I'll stop—I promise you.

Has our preaching been so shallow, our testimony so weak, our church services so tepid, our lives so apologetic that somehow we have communicated to our world that a person can give his life to Christ and still live in the gutter? We have allowed such cheap grace and such easy salvation to usher people into the Kingdom. We have forgotten to tell them that to give one's life to Christ means he gets all of that person's life. Paul says, "Old things are passed away; behold, all things are become new" (2 Cor. 5:17). There is a change or there's never been a salvation experience.

Burden Is More Than Buildings

Thirdly, Paul preached that a burden is better than a building. Consider all the buildings of Athens such as the agora, the marketplace, where men sat around and lodged new ideas upon the wings of discussion. There were famous buildings for gratifying the curiosity of the idle, unbelievable places where men gathered to share their so-called intellectual ideas. There was the Areopagus, the bema, where Paul preached, and, of course, the Parthenon, the temple of Athena, and the Epicureans where the seven virgin deities were beautifully carved out of limestone. The city of Athens had been built upon this center of intelligentsia. There were so many buildings and statues that, according to the Bible in Acts 17:23, the people built an altar "to the unknown god." They had gods, gods, gods everywhere, and they finally ran out of gods, so they built an altar to the "unknown" god.

Paul probably said, "Folks, listen. When you run out of names for god, you are too religious." That's what he said. And America is too religious. It is worshiping anything and everything except who it should worship.

But do you know why the Athenians built those buildings? Those buildings were built to appeal to the aesthetic appreciation of their deity. In other words, when they built the building, it was never to accommodate worshipers. In fact, some of those huge buildings wouldn't hold very many people because they were too full of statues of gods. Those large, imposing buildings were built so that the god could look down and say, "My, what a beautiful building you have built for me!"

But the real God doesn't need a building. What God wants in you and me is a *burden*. A building ought to be built as a place to reach people who are lonely, needy, and hungry, and who need to know the gospel of Jesus Christ.

I was preaching in Germany not long ago to an evangelism conference. I saw many of the great buildings and the magnificent cathedrals. A lady was showing me through one of the cathedrals, and I remarked, "This is a beautiful building." The lady said, "Oh, it's magnificent!" She began to tell me how fantastically beautiful and how old the building was. I then said something I probably shouldn't have. I said, "May I ask you a question?" She replied, "Anything." So I asked, "How many were saved here last Sunday?" She said, "Now, Sir, I don't know the answer to that."

Even after seeing those majestic buildings and great monuments to architectural accomplishment, nothing compares to the thrill I received when I came back to our church that next Sunday and had a little black boy, a little brown boy, and several men and women come to Jesus.

That was the same Sunday a prostitute came to trust Jesus. My wife, Sandy, was on the front row witnessing to her, and I'll never forget, as long as I live, watching as my wife wept out of compassion. A tear just seemed to hang on the end of Sandy's nose as her heart literally broke for that woman. As Sandy began to witness to her, I saw that prostitute pray, "Dear God, come into my heart. Come into my heart, Jesus. Save me." When they finished the prayer, both my wife and the newborn woman began to smile. I knew that here was an ex-prostitute who just that moment had been a work of God's miraculous grace. In the sight of God, that woman was now pure. God had made her clean by his grace. As I looked at the faces of that woman, that little black boy, that brown boy, and those men and women, I said, "That's what is beautiful to God." Not brick and mortar, not steeples or chandeliers or carpet. What's beautiful to God is men and women being saved, being born into the kingdom of God.

A burden is better than a building. The only reason for a building is to fill it with a burden.

Several years ago a little boy in Chicago was asked, "Why do you pass so many churches to come to Dwight L. Moody's church?" That little boy said, "Because at Mr. Moody's church they love little boys." We don't need anyone at our door saying, "You're not fit to be in here. You're not dressed right to be here. You don't smell right to be here." But, praise God, if we deserved to be here, we wouldn't need the Lord Jesus. We're here by his grace and by his love. That's the only reason we are here.

Earth Is Related to Eternity

Fourthly, the people to whom Paul preached thought the gospel of Christ was strange because Paul preached that *earth was related to eternity.* When Paul preached on the resurrection, the Bible says, they mocked. In Acts 17:31 Paul said, "Because he hath appointed a day, in the which he will judge the world in righteousness by that man whom he hath ordained; whereof he hath given assurance unto all men, in that he hath raised him from the dead." But they scoffed, and some mocked according to verse 32. Others said, "We will hear thee again of this matter."

Lost people die in a burning hell. Saved people go to a glorious heaven. Earth *is* related to eternity. What we do upon this earth has everything to do with how we will live in eternity. Don't forget that. You will, in the next breath, stand before the judgment bar of God. What the lost do on this earth affects eternity.

This is also true for the saved. The Bible says there will be a crown of life given to the martyrs who have died for Christ and a crown of glory given to those with the shepherding ministry. There is a crown of righteousness for those who look forward to the second coming.

There is a crown of rejoicing to be given to soul-winners. There is a crown incorruptible for those who have kept their bodies pure from sexual sins.

On that day will be those millions of precious martyrs dressed in white who died in the coliseums while being beheaded, who died at the guillotine, who died as their blood reddened the mouths of the lions in those distant arenas. They will all be there upon the shores of eternity and look over and see Jesus Christ. We'll know those crowns don't belong to us and we'll go to him and bow down to his blessed feet and put those crowns there and cry, "King of kings! Lord of lords!"

> All hail the pow'r of Jesus' name!
> Let angels prostrate fall;
> Bring forth the royal diadem,
> And crown him Lord of all.
> Bring forth the royal diadem,
> And crown him Lord of all.

> EDWARD PERRONET

Sometimes the child of God will be called a babbler. The gospel will be called strange. But don't worry about it. The world doesn't get to vote on you. You've just got one to please—the Lord God of heaven.

The world is bad, but remember that Paul said, "For I reckon that the sufferings of this present time are not worthy to be compared with the glory which shall be revealed in us" (Rom. 8:18).

When I was a little boy, my parents couldn't afford to buy a bicycle for me. At age fourteen I still didn't have a bicycle. A dear lady in our church by the name of Marie Black gave us a bicycle. It didn't have any fenders, chain guard, or handle grips. It was somewhat broken-down, but my dad and I worked on it. Finally, we got it repaired.

Not long afterwards, my dad went over to the East Grand area of Dallas to a Western Auto store. He didn't want me to go with him, but, at my insistence, he finally allowed me to go. My dad was at the service desk filling out some papers and browsing through the store when I found some handle grips wrapped in clear plastic marked, "99ᶜ." They had red, blue, and green plastic streamers coming out of them. I really wanted a pair of handle grips, so I went to my dad and said, "Daddy, can I have these handle grips? Daddy, I sure want them. They are only ninety-nine cents." He said, "No, Son, put them back." I said, "But, Dad, my handlebars are so slick and when my hands get sweaty, they slide off and I can't ride my bicycle very well. Daddy, I need some handle grips." He said, "Son, Daddy doesn't have the money. Now, go put them back." I said, "But, Daddy, they're only ninety-nine cents." Then he really got my attention because he said, "Bailey Eugene!" When my dad called me by my middle name, I knew I was in trouble.

We went back to East Dallas that day and I sat over in the car like a bullfrog, not saying a thing. On the way home, my dad tried to make conversation with me, but I said nothing.

The next day I came in from school and there in our living room, propped up on a kickstand was a brand-new Western Flyer bicycle. My grandmother lived with us, but I didn't think she could ride it, and I didn't know what it was doing there. My mother was seated on the couch with my daddy. My mother started dabbing her face with her handkerchief as tears came down her face. My eyes got so big as I stared at that bicycle with a little horn you could mash and brakes that made lights come on.

My daddy came over and put his big arm around my shoulder and said, "Son, while you were trying to bother me yesterday about those handle grips, I was ordering you this brand-new bicycle." I said, "Daddy, I'm so sorry for the way I acted. I'm so sorry."

I learned a valuable lesson. When God says no to one of his children today, it's because he's got a more glorious yes to say tomorrow. Wait upon the Lord, and you will mount up with wings. Whatever the world calls you, don't worry. We'll understand it better by and by.

6
Four Plus One Equals Zero

In Mark 10:17-22 we find the story of the rich young ruler.

> And when he was gone forth into the way, there came one running, and kneeled to him, and asked him, Good Master, what shall I do that I may inherit eternal life? And Jesus said unto him, Why callest thou me good? there is none good but one, that is, God. Thou knowest the commandments, Do not commit adultery, Do not kill, Do not steal, Do not bear false witness, Defraud not, Honour thy father and mother. And he answered and said unto him, Master, all these have I observed from my youth. Then Jesus beholding him loved him, and said unto him, One thing thou lackest: go thy way, sell whatsoever thou hast, and give to the poor, and thou shalt have treasure in heaven: and come, take up the cross, and follow me. And he was sad at that saying and went away grieved: for he had great possessions.

There were good things that this rich young ruler did. He was a young, bright, exciting, and intelligent man. There were at least four tremendously significant, noble, and worthwhile things that this young man did.

He came to Jesus when a person ought to come to Jesus. One ought to come to Jesus as soon as one knows and understands one is a sinner. The rich young ruler came to Jesus as a young person. The finest thing for one to do is to come to Christ at the earliest possible moment. Once a person understands that one is in sin, has rebelled against God, knows right from wrong, and knows that there is no hope in the world other than through Christ, one should come to Christ, whatever one's age.

The rich young ruler did a great thing by coming to Jesus when he was young. I remember preaching a revival in Arkansas while still in college. I got back to the dormitory room and several guys said, "Smith, what kind of revival did you have?" I said, "We had a great meeting. We had a seventy-year-old man saved." They rejoiced in that. I thought, *What a tremendous thing. This man had been hearing preachers for seventy years and had never gotten saved until I came along. I'm nineteen years old and he heard me at seventy and was saved.* I turned out the light and went to bed, but in a few moments, got back up, turned the lights back on, and apologized to those I had just talked with. I forgot to tell them that in the same revival a little nine-year-old boy had also accepted Jesus Christ as Savior.

Sometimes in revival meetings young children accept Christ and people say, "They don't know what they are doing. They must have all followed each other." That has happened, of course. But when I think of that seventy-year-old man coming to Christ and the nine-year-old boy, I say to myself, "What is so great about wasting sixty-nine years of your life? What is so great about living most of your life for the devil? What is so great about giving the devil the years of your life when your eyes were bright, when you could hear well, when you were young and exciting and vigorous? Why give the devil all those good, noble, upright years when you were healthy, and then come to Jesus as a fire escape? Brother, the best time to come to Jesus is nine years of age, not seventy! Don't waste your life."

Young people often say, "I don't want to be a Christian when I'm young. I've got all these exciting things to

do. I want to live it up. I think you have to be a sissy to
be a Christian when you are a young person." Don't ever
believe that. Some of the greatest athletes who have
ever lived have been men who loved God and were committed to Jesus Christ. Roger Staubach is a great Christian. Paul Anderson, called the strongest man in the
world, is a great Christian. He walks out on stage, gets
his back under a platform, and lifts nine preachers up in
the air. That is a lot of preachers! (Probably most of
them are overweight, too.) Paul Anderson lifts nine of
them with his back and says to the thousands at those
vast Billy Graham crusades, "If the strongest man in the
world needs Jesus Christ, then so do you." Don't ever
say it takes a sissy to be a Christian. It takes a man.

Even people who do not claim Jesus as Lord say that,
undoubtedly, Jesus Christ is the greatest man who ever
lived. If that is so, then the more one is like Jesus, the
more of a *man* he is. To whatever degree one is not like
Jesus Christ of Nazareth, he falls that much short of
what a man ought to be—because Jesus is the ultimate.
Jesus is the pattern. Jesus is the example, and to whatever extent we do not measure up to him, we are that
much *not* a man.

I went to school with Bill Glass who played with the
Cleveland Browns and Detroit Lions. Bill has big shoulders and big hands. I remember being told that I had big
hands, but when I shook hands with Bill Glass the first
time, I wondered what happened to my hand. It got lost
somewhere in his hand. No one would walk up to Bill
Glass and say, "Bill, I think you have to be a sissy to be a
Christian."

The rich young ruler came when a person ought to
come—when he was young. I have had people say to me,
"I wasted those young years of my life, and I would give

anything if I had given them to Christ." The time to come to Jesus is the time when a person is young, with the best years ahead of and not behind. Why give the devil, who hates us, the best years of our lives, and give God those little leftover years somewhere in the future?

Some want to sow wild oats and pray for a crop failure. Those wild seeds that are sown are going to take their toll upon that person and leave their mark.

Years ago I watched a newsreel of young boys marching in Moscow Square. There were thousands of them, and they had uniforms much like our Boy Scouts with the red bandanas around their necks. They were saying, "We will live. We will fight. We will die for our country." They were young boys—twelve, thirteen, or fourteen years of age—but they were willing to die for the Communist party. Hitler understood it, and Communism has understood it. To win the minds of the young is to have the generations that are to come.

We must not forget the older and the middle-aged people, but the greatest time to come to Jesus is in youth. If you have already wasted years, don't waste one more day. Don't waste one more night. You will never be any younger than you are now.

The rich young ruler came the way he should have come. The way to come to Jesus is in the right attitude and the right spirit. The Bible says the rich young ruler came running and knelt down. Looking up, he said, "Good Master." He had never called anyone "Good Master," for he was the master. He was the ruler. He knew Jesus had something that no one else could give and the rich young ruler did a good thing when he came to Jesus saying, "Master."

The running, kneeling, and the looking up indicate that he was humble. We are worthless people. We are people without hope; we are sinners. What man has to offer God is not nearly as much as what God has to offer man.

We Americans get so cocky because we live in good homes, drive good automobiles, and wear good clothes. When a preacher goes to South America and preaches, people flood down the aisles to be saved. They don't have a penny in their pockets. They are not leaning upon their riches! They know they don't have any hope in the world, and unless America becomes humble, God will make us poor again. God can bring us to our knees, and the only way we are going to come to Christ is to get a little more humble than we are right now. We have to be broken. Some of us are going to have to fall on our faces and say, "God, I'm nothing but a worthless sinner, and I need to know you as Savior." We have to come that way.

When I was pastor of a little country church, a member took me out one day to see his wheat fields. He said, "I want you to see my beautiful wheat." I said, "That wheat is wilted. It is all bent over at the top." We were riding in his pickup truck and he looked over at me as if to say, "You dummy." He said, "Preacher, you weren't brought up in the country, were you?" I said, "No, sir, I was raised in Dallas." He said, "That wheat that you see bending over is bending over because the kernel is full of wheat. It is bending over with the weight of its head. The wheat that is sticking straight up is tall and straight because the head is not heavy. It is empty." In the Christian life, those who hold their heads the tallest and strut around like painted peacocks are often those who have the least chance of ever knowing the kingdom of God. When we find a person who has a full head and full heart, we will find him bent over with the knowledge of the fact that he is worthless apart from God. We will find that person is worth something in the eyes of God because God has placed his heart into that person's heart and his Son into that person's life. There is hope for that sort of person. If we are cocky, it is very hard to come to Jesus. Proverbs 29:1 says, "He that being often reproved hardeneth his neck, shall be suddenly destroyed, and that without remedy." A man who thinks he knows it all and a man whose heart is hard is the man God can't even speak to because he shuts God out. The rich young ruler came in a humble way. He just approached Jesus and said, "Lord, I need you."

He came to the person. Of all the people he could have gone to, the rich young ruler came to Jesus. Doubtless he had many political friends that could have advised him. He probably knew some investors or some of the boys down at the "club." Instead, he came to the right person. He came to Jesus.

Look at these two men. Here was a man with braided shoes and another man with sandals. Here was a man whose hands were smooth enough to wave a scepter, but he came to a man whose hands were calloused from wielding a hammer. Here was a man whose skin was white because he worked indoors, but he came to a carpenter whose skin was bronze from exposure to the sun. Here was a man who had a great education, but he came to a man who had never sat at the feet of the professors. If anything, it would seem that Jesus should have been coming to the rich young ruler, but instead, this rich young ruler came to the *right person*. He came to Jesus.

Some have tried to find all kinds of substitutes for Jesus. Some say, "I'll find my kicks in alcohol." I've lost relatives because of alcohol. We have a man in our church who trains state troopers. He has all of the statistics and he could tell you that the greatest enemy to mankind on our highways is alcohol. We license a person to fill up with alcohol, get on the highway, go the wrong way on a one-way street, have a head-on collision with an innocent, godly family, killing a wife, father, and child. That person may be in jail for two years, then will be let out to get drunk and possibly kill someone else. That is wrong in the eyes of God.

The insanity of our nation is that we cannot have Bible reading and prayer in school, but the kids can go around telling filthy jokes and getting drunk. Some have said, "We can get a six pack and have a good time." I know a lot of guys who are crippled because of a six pack. A boy in El Dorado, Arkansas, couldn't make a thirty-mile-an-hour curve at ninety miles an hour because he had about five beers in him. He lost his life. What a tragedy! When one is full of Jesus, one wants to enjoy everything there is about life.

Some find a substitute for Jesus in dope. A young girl in our church came to me heartbroken because the boy she was going to marry now has a sixth-grade mentality because of LSD. In Hobbs, New Mexico, a young girl had a backlash of LSD. They put her in the hospital and a young doctor from our church diagnosed her problem. That girl was having hallucinations on her hospital bed and saw all kinds of monsters on the ceiling. That dedicated, brilliant doctor said to me, "Pastor, if I could have taken every mother and father in this city into that girl's hospital room, and they could have watched her writhe and twist as if her body were lying naked on hot coals, there would not have been one parent in this city who would be soft on marijuana." She started out with just a little "pot" and ended up on LSD. Few people start with the hard stuff. They get into marijuana and on it goes.

In the July 8, 1974, edition of *Time*, there was an arti-

cle with a picture of some who said they had the answer
for all of us "fuddy-duddies" who believe in Jesus. They
were telling how one ought to be on marijuana. They
were from the University of California at Berkeley, a
great university of higher learning. They supposedly
"have the answer." That's where LSD advocate Timothy
Leary got his start. The guy who wrote the article had
some sense. He reported, "At age twenty-three,
_____ _____ has a thin, wasted face and the
appearance of a man twice his age. A welfare recipient,
he spends his days wandering down Telegraph Avenue
in Berkeley, California, with a bottle of cheap wine or a
marijuana cigarette in his hand. _____ _____,
twenty-one, also a Telegraph Avenue regular, earns a
scant forty dollars a month, mostly by selling his blood.
_____ _____, seventeen, lives off the refuse of
Berkeley garbage cans and occasionally peddles dope."
A few years ago, these were in the "In Group," but when
they reached their early twenties, they became nothing
but bums on skid row.

How did this generation of young "has-beens" come to
exist? "For some," say the researchers, "there were
serious family problems or limitations in psychological,
intellectual abilities of sublime or barely articulated
knowledge." I have three degrees myself, but I don't
understand that. When you put your life in Jesus Christ,
there is a new hope, a new joy, and a new existence. A
saved man will not want to ruin his body, but will want
to make his body a "living sacrifice, holy, acceptable
unto God, which is your reasonable service" (Rom. 12:1).
Any substitute for Jesus is bad. Some have made fun of
kids in the church who love to get excited about Jesus.
They say, "We are having harmless fun." But sin is
never harmless!

The rich young ruler asked the question he should have asked. He asked, "How do I get eternal life? How do I get saved? How do I go to heaven?" Van Cliburn, the great concert pianist, could go over to a piano, take some polish and shine that piano, but that's not the best thing Van Cliburn could do with a piano. Hank Aaron could take a needle and thread and sew up a baseball, but that's not the best thing he could do with a baseball. Billy Graham could get up and give a little devotional on Sunday night, but that's not the best thing Billy Graham could do with his time in sharing the Word of God.

Jesus might make a man happy, make him think positively, help him have an appreciation for art and literature, encourage him to go to church and have a nice little family, but the greatest thing Jesus Christ can do is lift a man from a devil's hell and give him a home in heaven. The rich young ruler did not come to Jesus asking secondary things. He came asking, "What shall I do that I may inherit eternal life?"

Some have only asked Jesus to help them cope with a particular situation. That's fine and good. But when one skips first base, one is completely out.

Someone asked John Wesley how he found salvation apart from the Anglican Church. The founder of the Methodist Church said, "I was on a ship one time during a terrible storm and some Moravian missionaries on board were not afraid. I *was* afraid and they looked at me and said, 'Mr. Wesley, why are you afraid?' I said, 'Why are you *not* afraid?' They said, 'We know Christ. Mr. Wesley, do you know Christ?' When they looked at me and said that, I could only say, 'I know the Church, I know the creeds, but I don't know Christ.' " We must all ask Jesus that ultimate question, "What must I do to be saved?"

The rich young ruler came to Jesus when a person ought to come. He came the way he ought to come, came to the person he should come to, and he asked the question he must ask. When Jesus gave him the answer, he went away sad and did not do what Jesus said. The four good things he did, plus the one fact that when all was said and done, he refused to be obedient to Jesus, equals absolutely zero.

Jesus probably didn't want him to give up all his money. He only wanted him to be willing to. Jesus wanted his trust. People need not fear what is going to happen when they trust Jesus. Some have some unbelievable, untrue fears. Jesus wants us to trust him and place ourselves in his arms because his arms have never dropped anyone.

7
The Five M's of the New Birth

There's probably no phrase in religious circles that has become more prominent of late than the phrase, "born again." Everyone is writing about it. Billy Graham has had a best-seller, *How to Be Born Again*, and Charles Colson has written about it.

In John 3:3 Jesus told Nicodemus, "Verily, verily, I say unto thee, Except a man be born again, he cannot see the kingdom of God." Many people confuse what Jesus is saying and believe that the phrase "being saved" is a Baptist phrase.

A Catholic girl once told me, "Catholics get baptized. Baptists get saved." But we need to realize that everyone who goes to heaven gets "saved," "repents," and is "born again."

Former President Carter made the phrase, born again, well known. Many people assume if you are born again, you are a Baptist. It would be a great thing if every Baptist *were* born again, but every "Baptist" is *not* born again. There won't be any denominational tags such as Catholic, Presbyterian, Assembly of God, Pentecostal, Methodist, or Baptist in heaven. In heaven there will only be people who have been *born again*.

If a man is not born again, he is one heartbeat from hell. Jesus said, "Except a man be born again, he cannot see the kingdom of God." I don't care how formally, wonderfully, and interestingly you got into a Lutheran, Catholic, or Baptist church—if you've not been born again, you are not a Christian.

There is a great deal of difference between catechism and being saved. There is a great deal of difference between confessionals and being born again. The real issue is what Jesus asked. "Have you been born again?"

Let's examine five "M's" of the new birth. Over 50,000,000 Americans claim to have been born again. If so many claim this, it is important that we seek to understand what the Bible really says about being "born again."

First, we need to think about the *man* of the new birth. In John 3, a man who was a ruler came to Jesus Christ. Not only was he a ruler, he was also a wealthy, intelligent Jew. But an intelligent man is not necessarily an enlightened man. There are many men who have Ph.D.'s and a lot of learning, but they have never known what it is to be enlightened.

Here was a man who was a ruler, but he was not saved. Not only was he a ruler, but he was equal to a pastor of a large church. He was a Pharisee and very spiritual, yet Jesus looked at him and said, "Nicodemus, you've got to be born again."

What's great about knowing Christ is that when you come to know him, he doesn't simply take the old garment of your life and put a new patch on it. Jesus said you can't put a new patch on an old garment any more than you can put new wine in old wineskins. Jesus Christ gives you a whole new garment! A whole new life!

Being saved is not getting a "new patch." The Bible says Jesus Christ himself grew mentally, spiritually, physically, and emotionally. If you don't grow like that, you've never been born again because being born again means becoming a whole new person.

When a child is born, the news doesn't come out in the

paper that, "The head was born at 8:04; the right arm was born at 8:06; and the left arm was born at 8:30." No! That would be a terrible way to be born. When a child is born, he is born! Some people say, "Well, I've got my *mind* with God," or, "I've got my body with God," or, "I've got my emotions with God," or, "I've got my finances with God." That cannot be.

Mankind is sinful, and we have to be born again because it is our nature to sin. But when Christ comes into our lives, we get new bodies, new lives, and new experiences. Everything is new about us.

When we're born again, everything is changed. We're made different. A United States senator from another state came to the church to hear me preach, but wouldn't join because he was afraid of the severity with which I preached and the truth I preached from the Word of God. Once I referred to him in a message, and called him a compromiser. He came to see me and said, "Preacher, you were referring to me last Sunday on the radio. You don't like it that I drink, do you?" And I said, "No, Sir." "You don't like it because I have some standards other than what you have, do you?" he continued. I said, "No, Sir." He said, "Bailey Smith, don't you know that I'm not a really bad guy?" I looked at him and said, "Jack, that's right. You are not a bad guy. You are just going to go to hell."

It's not that "good" people go to heaven and "bad" people go to hell. It's not that people are bad, they are just *lost*. You do not come to Jesus Christ as a senator; you must come to Jesus Christ as a *sinner*.

The second "M" is the word *must*. Someone once asked Charles Finney, "Why do you always preach on the subject, 'You must be born again'?" I love his answer. He said, "I preach on it a lot because you *must* be born again." That's a good answer. Jesus said, "Nicodemus, you *must* be born again." Why *must?* Because Romans 3:23 says, "All have sinned, and come short of the glory of God." Isaiah 53:6 says that all of us have drifted away from God. "There is none righteous, no, not one" (Rom. 3:10). Isaiah 59:2 says, "But your iniquities have separated between you and your God, and your sins have hid his face from you, that he will not hear."

Let me list deadly sins: (1) pleasure without conscience; (2) cleverness without character; (3) science without humanity; (4) wealth without work; (5) industry without morality; (6) politics without principle; (7) religion without reality. But remember, any sin is deadly unless you are born again.

It doesn't matter how important we are or how religious we are. Some have religion, but they don't have Jesus. Religion without Jesus Christ is damnable.

Some say, "The devil made me do it." The devil has never made us do anything we did not want to do. The reason we have sinned in the past is because we flatly enjoyed it! People commit sins of immorality because they have pleasure and sensual fulfillment from them. Why does a man take that bottle? Because he enjoys it. Why does man make that money through crooked business dealings? Because he enjoys it! Why will a man eat until he becomes overweight? Because he enjoys it. The reason man enjoys sin is because, by nature, man is a sinner.

There's a third "M" of being born again which I call *misconception.* A lot of people think they are all right because they had a great mom and dad. That's good, but they themselves must be born again.

A lady said to me a few months ago, "Brother Bailey,

I'm a Methodist. What do I have to do to join First Southern?" I said, "Get saved." She said, "Well, you don't believe Methodists are lost, do you?" I said, "No, I don't believe that Methodists are any more lost than Baptists are lost. If you've been saved, your salvation is just as good as a Baptist salvation. But I want you to know that you can't just come join our church unless you've been saved." I request our staff to ask all who come for membership if they have been saved—even preachers.

Some think just because they have had good backgrounds, everything is going to be all right. But being born again means there has been a time when one has invited Jesus into his life and committed himself to Christ.

The fourth "M" is the word *meaning*. What is the meaning of the new birth? Here are some references for the meaning of being born again. First Peter 1:22, which says a born-again person will love. First John 3:9 says a saved man will not be living in sin. James 1:27 says the child of God will be unspotted by the world. When a person gives his life to being born again, he will have those characteristics.

The fifth "M" is the word *master*. I've learned something about a person who has been born again. That person is willing to obey the Word of God.

When a person gets saved, he gets a new family. I don't have a large earthly family, but I'm part of the family of God. God is my Father; Jesus is my elder brother; the Holy Spirit is my constant companion. The Lord and I have a special relationship, and we can say good-bye to the devil now and forevermore.

Jesus is the "author and finisher of our faith" (Heb. 12:2). The reason some have not had their faith finished or completed is because Jesus has never been the author of their lives. He has to be the author before he can be the finisher. Remember what Jesus said would happen if we have not been born again: we will not see the kingdom of God. You cannot go to heaven unless you have been born again. You are born again by asking Jesus to come into your life. If you ask him to save you, he will. It's not by feeling. If you could be saved by feelings, God wouldn't have given us the Bible. He's given us the Bible to tell us how to be saved, and Romans 10:13 says: "For whosoever shall call upon the name of the Lord shall be saved."

If you want to be saved, pray this prayer right now, "Dear God, forgive me of my sins. I want to be saved. I give my heart to you. Now, thank you, Jesus, for saving me. In Jesus' name I pray. Amen."

8
The Unanswerable Question

Let me ask you a question that you will not be able to answer. Not even all the demons of hell or the devil himself could answer this one. The cherubim, the seraphim of heaven or any other angel could not answer it either. It is a question to which not even God himself has given us an answer.

In actuality, the Bible poses many questions. In Genesis 3:9, "The Lord God called unto Adam, and said unto him, Where art thou?" A little later the Bible records Cain asking, "Am I my brother's keeper?" (Gen. 4:9). Job asked, "If a man die, shall he live again?" (14:14). Mark 8:37 records yet another question that ought to be asked. "What shall a man give in exchange for his soul?" The previous verse says, "For what shall it profit a man, if he shall gain the whole world and lose his own soul?" Simon Peter asks in 1 Peter 4:17, "What shall be the end of them that obey not the gospel of God?"

We can ponder all of these questions. In fact, most of them can be answered because the Bible answers them. But, I'm going to ask you a question that you cannot answer. All the power of hell cannot answer it. Even all the wisdom of heaven cannot answer it. It is a great question, but it has no answer.

The Bible has 1,189 chapters. Three of them tell man where he came from, and 1,186 tell him where he is going. The Bible is a road map to eternity. It is a directive toward destiny.

Let's examine Hebrews 2:3. Here we find a question

for which there is no answer. However, it is a question
that we must ask. "How shall we escape, if we neglect so
great salvation?" This is an unanswerable question.

In the next few pages we shall take this powerful
Scripture, and consider it phrase by phrase to see what
message God has for us.

Implication of Impossibility

First of all, please notice the phrase, "How shall," and
its implication of impossibility. We see nothing but the
utter futility, the hopelessness, and the frustration that
is in the mind of the writer of Hebrews. "How shall," or
"How can." We can sense the fact that, as he asks the
question, he knows no answer. He knows that in all the
universe of God, even if man comes with great powers of
inspection, discovery, or clairvoyance, that he will not
be able to find an answer. We can observe despair well-
ing up in the man who asks the question, "How can?"

He asked the question, knowing even before he fin-
ishes the sentence that it is much like asking, "How can a
man toss a mountain over the sun?" "How can a child
touch a star?" "How can a baby tutor his father in
physics?" "How can an animal relate the theory of rela-
tivity?" "How can a salmon stretch its fins and fly to the
moon?" "How can a dwarf leap to the top of the Eiffel
Tower?" "How can a sparrow topple the Rock of Gibral-
tar?"

We might as well search for a man with gills and a fish
with lungs as to search for an answer to the question,
"How can we escape if we neglect so great salvation?" It
is impossible to discover an answer to this query.

Inclusion of Every Individual

Notice a second word in the Scripture which indicates
inclusion of every individual. "How shall *we?*" This en-

compasses every one of us: the erudite scholar and the illiterate; the extroverted socialite and the island recluse; the busy businessman and the paralytic; the Pope and the parishioner; the church member and the saloon keeper; the virtuous woman and the prostitute; the man of wealth and the man of poverty; the man of eloquence and the man with a speech impediment—every person on the face of the earth is included in this question that cannot be answered. "How shall *we?*"

On May 25, 1979, a DC-10 airplane, weighing over 300 tons, took off from Chicago's O'Hare Field going to Los Angeles. After a few seconds of flight, the aircraft lost one of its left engines, turned to the right, and crashed upside down, killing all 272 passengers.

Aboard there was a man and wife who worked for a famous "girlie" magazine. She had just written a new book. Two other passengers were on the staff of the same magazine. Immediately some might say, "God took Flight #191, and he brought his wrath upon that pornographic organization by the death of this man, his wife, and his assistants."

I don't think that's true, for also on that airplane was a doctor from South Carolina who had delivered over 2,000 babies. He was a man who loved God. June 12 was scheduled to be "Dr. Day" in his hometown. He was on his way to a medical meeting in Tahiti, but he never made the meeting. He never came back for his day in his hometown.

We must be careful in saying that the plane crashed because of the wrath of God upon the porno personnel. The last sentence of the article published by Associated Press that related the story of the most devastating, costly crash in the history of American aviation was this, "There were no survivors. Two hundred seventy-two people perished."

The preacher, the priest, the Christian, the little baby, the little girls, the beautiful women, the handsome men, the scholarly, the people who had planned for retirement and were depending on the plane to get them to the places they had already purchased, all died. Everyone perished.

When the judgment of God falls upon the prostitute, it will fall upon the drunk, the thief, the adulterer, the agnostic, and the atheist. But, if we think that God will stop there, we are wrong. When the wrath of God falls, there will be no survivors. The self-righteous, the church member, the priest . . . all will fall. Everyone who has never totally committed his life to Christ will be included. Those who have tried to escape this salvation or have tried some way other than the blood of Christ will be included. Those who have tried to steal their way into heaven by baptism, by church membership, by works—all of these will perish. When the wrath of God falls, it will not only be on the noticeably wicked, such as the Hitlers and Mussolinis and Stalins of this world; it will be on everyone who has tried to get to God by some way other than through Christ.

Notice the word *we*. There will be no survivors. When the judgment of God falls on those who are left after the coming of Christ, there will be no survivors.

Insistence On Incarceration

Thirdly, the next word to consider is "escape." I call this "the insistence on incarceration." To be incarcerated is to be placed behind bars. It is to be arrested, put in prison, locked up. The Bible indicates that those who have never been born again are incarcerated.

Do you realize that man has within himself the very

ingredient of his eternal destruction? There is not one thing a man has to do to die and go to hell. He must do something to go to heaven, but the natural result of man's rebellion against God and his fallen nature is that he is locked up. Man is a captive to his own nature.

For example, it is the nature of a dog to bark, a cat to meow, a cow to moo, and it is man's nature to sin. It is man's nature to turn his back upon God. We never spank a child to get him to do bad. A child does that without trying. We must discipline a child to get him to be good. Why? Because a child already has a rebellious nature. He likes to flex his own independent muscles. He decides to be selfish. He decides to be greedy. He is, by nature, a rebel, a sinner. Because of this, we are incarcerated. We are enslaved. You ask, "Why?" Because the Bible says that we must escape. Escape what? Escape our sinful nature. In Christ, old things are passed away, all things are become new.

We must escape the judgment of God. Listen! We might run from God all of our lives, but one day we will stand before his throne.

Let me interject some food for thought. How is a man going to escape hell? When that DC-10 airplane crashed, it was carrying 20,000 gallons of jet fuel. When it exploded, those around said the flames shot 300 to 400 feet into the air. A priest was allowed to examine the charred bodies. They picked the people up in plastic bags. How did the lost escape?

I flew in an airplane not long after that incident, and I noticed the beautiful women and the handsome men as they passed by. I thought to myself that one particular lady was probably very much like someone on that DC-10. She was sharp. Her dress had been just the right length to be in style. She had worn the right high-heeled shoes. Her hair had been immaculately styled. Her nails were perfectly manicured. Her makeup was without flaw, and she had glistening hair, a crystal-clear complexion. Later, the priest said, "I could not distinguish the men from the women because of the badly burned bodies."

My friends, they were fastened by seat belts. They were in the airplane and they had no escape. But, listen carefully, they were as free as birds in comparison to a person who tries to escape hell apart from salvation through Jesus Christ!

Those people felt enslaved and captive in that airplane, but they were not nearly so captive as are those who have turned their backs upon Jesus Christ. I don't care how good a person is. I don't care how circumspectly a person lives. I don't care if a person has been through catechism, confession, or whatever! Has that person ever known Christ? Has he ever been born again? Has he ever known what it is to be saved? Has he ever known what it is to be converted? Has he ever known what it is to let Jesus set him free? The Bible says we are incarcerated. We are imprisoned. We are in need of escape if we've never known Jesus Christ as Savior.

A young Christian boy dated a girl who wasn't a Christian. He tried to witness to her, but she said, "Look, this is the 'now.' Let's just be concerned with the 'now.' Don't worry about whether I'm going to heaven or not. That's the 'hereafter.' It has nothing to do with what's going on here." He said, "Well, you are wrong. The 'hereafter' has a lot to do with what we do now. In fact, what we do here determines the 'hereafter.' " The hereafter begins in the "right now." The Bible says that if one doesn't escape, it will be because one did not trust in Jesus Christ.

We have seen the implication of impossibility in "How shall?" We have been made aware of the inclusion of every individual implied in the "we." We have examined the idea of the insistence on incarceration in "escape." Now, let us look at the little word *if*. The word *if* is in the Bible 1,522 times. However, it is never written with more power or loaded with more truth than it is right here. The word *if* brings us to the fourth point in our study. "The insanity of inaction." Please notice the word that follows "if." It is "neglect." Did you see that it is not "reject"? It is "neglect."

Insanity of Inaction

One doesn't have to burn his business in order to destroy it. One doesn't have to plant weeds in a garden in order to lose it. All one need do is neglect it. We don't have to beat our mates in order to ruin our marriages. Just neglect them. We don't have to hit ourselves with our fists to ruin our health. Just neglect it.

A man of the Niagara River does not have to row to the great chasm where he will fall to his death. The only thing he has to do is take his oars and put them in the boat. He does not have to paddle at all. He will go over the abyss to his death with absolutely no effort.

People do not have to outwardly mock God or reject the Holy Spirit by shaking their fists in his face. They do not actually have to do anything. They can just be good people. They can go to club meetings, serve on boards and committees, and be fine, upstanding, moral people. All that is necessary is to do *nothing* about spiritual things. The problem with America is not open hostility, it is passive indifference. I've never had anyone beat me because I am a preacher. I have never had anyone want to bomb one of the churches I was pastoring. They just let us go on preaching what we want to preach, doing what we want to do, having any starlight crusade we want to have, waving our Bibles any way we want, and they will go ahead doing what they want to do. The Bible says there will be no escape if there is neglect. "How shall we escape, if we neglect?"

At one time Paul conversed with a very important man in politics. His name was Felix. Felix was very polite to Paul. He listened to him with great interest. When Paul finished speaking, Felix said, "Well, Paul, I don't think I'll decide now. I'll tell you what, Paul. At a more convenient season, I'll call you." The Bible never tells us that Felix called for Paul again. He didn't beat him; he didn't stone him; he didn't arrest him; he just said, "Not now, Paul. Some other time."

A sailor deserves to be lost if he refuses a compass. A hungry man deserves to die of starvation if he rejects the bread that has been offered to him. Likewise, a man deserves to spend eternity in hell when he turns his back upon the love of God that takes away the sin of the world. Jesus did not intend to pay such a price for the sins of mankind and have mankind treat it so frivolously. Never! He did not walk up Golgotha's hill, and die on Calvary's cross, in order that man might be flippant. Anyone who neglects so great a salvation deserves to be lost.

A man and his son were fishing in the cold waters of a northern sea. They stood on a little ice tip that reached out into the water. If they had fallen into the freezing waters, they would have been instantly killed. But, again and again, they walked out on that frozen tip. They thought it was safe. Then, all of a sudden, the very tip of that little frozen part jutting out into the sea broke off. The boy and his father were sent sailing away from the mainland. The father said, "Son! You've only a second to think. Jump!" The father jumped to land and saved his life. But the boy, as if he were part of the frozen ice, hesitated until it was too late to jump. For some reason, he remained on the piece of ice as it floated out into the ocean. He was never seen again. He had neglected to jump. He wanted to! But, for some reason, he didn't. He was lost forever.

Infinity of the Invitation

Now, let's look at the last phrase, "so great salvation." Let's please notice the infinity of the invitation. Oh, I love the last phrase, "so great salvation." Why is it a great salvation? Here are five reasons.

First, it is great because of its donor. Who is the donor? Jehovah is the donor. The almighty God, the omnipotent God of heaven is the donor. Salvation was created in the councils of heaven. It is a great salvation because of the fact that God gave it.

Secondly, it is great because of its doctrine. I am so glad it is not a salvation of works because no one would make it. I am so greatful that we are not under the old legal system anymore, and that we don't have to die on a cross ourselves! It is a great salvation because it is not by works of righteousness which we have done, but by the precious blood of Jesus. He has washed us clean. It is a salvation by grace. It is not what we do, but what God has done for us. We only receive it. What a beautiful doctrine!

Thirdly, it is great because of its duration. An eternal God has an eternal salvation. God has saved us forever.

Fourthly, it is great because it is distinctive. Distinctive means unique; one of a kind. It is the *great* one because it is the *only* one. It is not the only religion, but it *is* the only salvation.

Last of all, it is great because of its donation. The other day I was with a group planning a picnic. A lady said, "One of you bring the salad. Another will bring the meat, and another will bring the dessert."

In another planning meeting, God was planning man's salvation. I can imagine the angels said, "We'll bring the message." The prophets said, "We'll donate the preaching." John the Baptist said, "I'll prepare the way." And God the Father said, "I'll give my Son." It is a great salvation because of its donation. Jesus Christ was donated by God in our behalf. Because of the donation of Christ, man can be saved.

Is the work of God in creation the greatest thing God ever did? I think not. The greatest thing is not creation, but re-creation. It is not generation, but rather, regeneration. You say, "Oh, Preacher, how about the different versions of the Bible?" It is not the versions God is concerned with. It is the conversions. You see, when the world was created, not one person shed a tear. There was not one drop of blood shed. But, when God re-created the world, the blood of his Son was shed, and Christ wept. What a price was paid!

Ah, here is a question we cannot answer. However, I do have tremendous good news. We can be saved from hell. We can go to heaven if we do not neglect this great salvation. God has offered it to the world—to you! Will you receive Jesus Christ today?

9
Ditches in the Desert

I would now like for us to examine the richness of 2 Kings 3. At the time of this passage, Mesha, the king of Moab was trying to outwit Jehoram, king of Israel. Israel, Judah, and Edom were upset because Mesha was not fulfilling his agreement to pay the king of Israel 100,000 lambs and the wool of 100,000 rams. Mesha had promised this to the former king of Israel, Ahab, before he died. But when Ahab died, Mesha backed out on the agreement. Because of this, Jehoram and the people were upset. They said, "We've been 'Christian' about this long enough! Now, we're going to fight. If he won't give us what we have coming . . . if he'll not give us what he agreed to, then we'll make war against him."

When they started doing this, they ran into an extremely interesting problem. I want us to see "floods of blessing in new ditches." Some of the experiences these people had would challenge the understanding of the so-called Sunday-morning crowd. However, there is also a deep message for those who are really up to date scripturally and spiritually. We will see some interesting facts about this story as the Israelites went to make war against the king of Moab.

If there is any passage in the Bible that excites me and helps me see what the church I pastor ought to be, and, if there is any passage in the Bible that is a reflecting mirror held up to my personal life, it is this one.

Notice, first of all, an urgent need that came to light.

The army was arrayed in full armor. From the tips of their toes to the tops of their heads, they were ready for war. Their swords were in hand, their tempers were flaring, their minds were made up, and they had their sense of direction. They had everything necessary to be victorious. One cannot imagine a people better organized, more militaristic, or more determined to be victorious than these people of Israel. And yet, as they started out into the battle, all of a sudden, they said, "Uh, oh, something is wrong. We forgot that we don't have any water."

Imagine that. What an unusual plight! These people had spared no expense at all in their organization or in their arrangement. They were complete in their regimentation. But, when they came to the valley where the battle was to begin, they discovered that, even though they were prepared to fight from a military standpoint, they did not have enough water to sustain the soldiers.

What a strange dilemma! What an intriguing truth! It is parabolic of the church in that the church is organized, it is functional, and it has done everything our denomination has suggested. But, it may not have the Spirit of the Living God. Whatever we do in organization, promotion, or advertising will be completely useless for victory unless we have the Water of Life. That is absolutely essential. These people went out prepared with most everything, but discovered they did not have one thing that was essential, water.

I remember seeing an old Western movie in which there was a tragic scene about a man dying on the desert with a pouch full of solid gold pieces. Given a choice, that man would have traded that sack of gold for a drink of water.

One of the things I love about First Southern Baptist

Church of Del City is the fact that while we may not have the most ornamental auditorium in America, I believe with all my heart that the members would rather have the Water of Life than a pouch of gold. Many of our churches may have chandeliers that cost fifty thousand dollars, but, if they really knew what they ought to be doing, they would trade them for the Water of Life to make their churches came alive.

The Israelite army had regimentation and weapons, everything outwardly necessary, but they discovered that they did not have the inward sustenance for life. Let us never forget that the real spiritual battle in which we are engaged is one in which we need God's presence more than anything else.

The Israelites were excited about winning the battle, but I'm so grateful for the fact that when they discovered they didn't have any water, they didn't look for a "water man." They didn't seek a geologist. They didn't seek out one of those funny guys with a crooked stick who walks along waving it over the ground, and all of a sudden goes, "Wheep!" and there is water. Who did they seek? Notice in verse 11: "But Jehoshaphat said, Is there not a prophet of the Lord here, that we may enquire of the Lord by him?" And a servant answered and said, Here's Elisha."

I want you to note that the word *prophet* is not capitalized. Each of us can be a prophet of God. Whatever the lost think of us—whether they think we are great in innovation, ingenuity, or promotion, or whether we are great at being clever in manipulation of organizations—I hope they will think of us when they need people of God. I only hope they will call on a member of the church of Jesus Christ.

We may be entertaining, and we may have a sensational program, but when people have needs, and the water runs dry, and the well gets shallow, they will look for a person who has been close to God. That's what these Israelites looked for. "Where's the preacher? Where's the prophet? Where's the person who can give us a word from God?"

When I became pastor of First Southern, it was a most humbling experience. I've never walked before that congregation to preach unless I've spent some time on my knees in prayer moments before the service. You see, more than anything else, I want people to see and hear a man who has been with God, a man who has been on his knees before God.

Dwight L. Moody used to preach massive crusades. When it was time for him to preach, if he didn't know that God was ready for him to preach, he'd tell his music director to sing another song. That's the way a man of God ought to be. "Sing another song. I'm not ready. I'm not bathed enough. I'm not cleansed enough. The Spirit of God is not upon me enough. I need more of God's power before I stand before God's people."

When the need came and the thirst came, the people said, "Where's the man of God?" I want our church, more than anything else, to be known around our state and around the nation as a source of spiritual advice when needs come. For example, when a true revival of the Spirit needs to come, they can call here from any congregation in America and ask us to pray with them for help from God. That is the desire of my heart.

"Where is the prophet? Where is the prophet of God?" That's what Israel wanted.

Notice the message they received in verses 16-17. Elijah said to them, "Thus saith the Lord." Every prophet ought to start out like that, shouldn't he? "Make this valley full of ditches. For thus saith the Lord, Ye shall not see wind, neither shall ye see rain; yet that valley shall be filled with water, that ye may drink, both ye, and your cattle, and your beasts"

Have you ever known anyone who thinks things would be better if they could just move? If she didn't have the husband she has . . . if he didn't have the wife he has . . . if they didn't have the children they have, things would be better. If the pews were softer, the windows more beautiful, the choir a little louder, the preacher a little softer . . . everything would be better. Have you ever known anyone like that?

In this passage, the prophet of God says, "Dig ditches where you are because God is about to do something. But, he isn't going to do it if he has to do it the way you think he should." That's right! He said, "You're not going to see rain; you are not going to see wind, but you are going to see water." He said, "God isn't going to do anything for you unless he does it through a miracle."

We don't need to operate churches in a haphazard manner. There is a man in our church whom I appreciate more every day. He's got an analytical mind. That man is constantly devising ways for the church to save money and pay off part of our debt. He just thinks that way. First Southern ought to operate in a businesslike manner. But there comes a time when a church has to work according to the miracle God wants to do for it. That's the bottom line.

If we trust natural causes, or if we trust circumstances to bring God's work about, we are going to become a mediocre, dried-up church, and God will seldom bless us. But, when we say to the world, "Watch out, God's going to do a miracle at First Southern Baptist Church," then we'd better dig the ditches. Elisha commanded, "Dig the ditches. There's work to be done in the valley." If we want to have everything in *our* order, and have everything to tally up to *our* standards, we will remain the same. We can be a well-orginized "people's church," but when we become "God's church," we'd better dig the ditches. Listen to the prophet, "You're not going to see any reason for water to come. There's not going to be any wind or rain. There's not going to be a lot of folderol to it. It's going to be a miracle."

Notice that important word *yet* in verse 17. We need to draw a circle around it. It shows us that even though one and three may not seem to make five, God is going to work it out that way. Elisha said, "I'm going to show you a miracle. Indeed, there's going to be water here."

You say, "Preacher, how do you really apply that?" Well, I think there are several ways we can apply this Scripture to our personal lives. First of all, we ought to commit more than we have to God. Secondly, we ought to submit more than we have to God. Thirdly, we ought to operate our Christian lives on the basis of faith. The Bible says it is impossible to please God without faith. If we have everything in our Christian lives all figured out, if we already know where every penny is coming from that we give to the church, if we know where all our time is going to come from that we are going to spend in witnessing next year, if we know how we are going to fulfill the commitments that we have made to our committees, then we are not pleasing to God. We can only be pleasing to God when our lives so far exceed our abilities that we have to depend on him to accomplish the task. We cannot be pleasing to God unless this is the case. It is impossible to please God without faith.

Why dig ditches in the valley? The reason is: God said to. This is where the blessings are going to come. My friend, what I'm asking of you is to get ready for what God is going to do. Prepare! If you're not prayed up, pray up. If you haven't submitted as you ought to, submit. If you're not committed as you ought to be, commit. If you're not dedicated to God as he requires, then become dedicated. Unless the ditches are dug, you're going to be left high and dry. That's right! God challenges, "Get ready. The water is going to come."

Have you ever missed a blessing of God because you weren't ready? I have. I've heard preachers whom I've criticized, instead of receiving a blessing, because my heart did not have ditches in the valley. I admit it. I've heard music and didn't receive a blessing, and I have criticized that music because I had not been digging ditches in the valley. I wasn't ready for what God wanted to pour upon me and do in my life. God said, "Get ready." Wouldn't it be terrible if God wanted to do something miraculous in our churches, and we weren't ready for it? The waters would come upon us, but they would not be held because we had not dammed up the places where God wanted to give us water. We didn't get ready to store up spiritual blessings. Wouldn't that be horrible?

I had an uncle who was a terrific fisherman. I often wondered why we could be in the same boat, and he'd catch all the fish and I wouldn't catch even one. One day I looked in his tackle box, and I understood. Man, he had everything in the world that could catch a fish. I believe he could have caught any fish in existence. I think even if that fish had just eaten a turkey dinner, he'd still bite. Why? Because my uncle had all kinds of funny-looking lures, flys, and hooks. He was ready for every circumstance. I've often seen him take one hook off and put a lure on. He would do everything he could, with everything he had. He was ready!

I believe God wants to do something in our land, don't you? I want us to be ready. Whatever it is, I want us to be ready to launch out on faith. He said, "Yet, I'm going to bring a great blessing upon you."

Verse 13 states: "Elisha said unto the king of Israel, What have I to do with thee? get thee to the prophets of thy father, and to the prophets of thy mother, And the king of Israel said unto him, Nay: for the Lord hath called these three kings together, to deliver them into the hand of Moab."

This Scripture is revealing. This king had never served the living God, and yet he wanted the prophet of God to help him with this water problem. Sometimes we discover that people who will not even speak to us will come to us when a time of crisis occurs in their lives. When it is time for God to deal in their lives, they are going to call on us.

This is why I have determined never to shut a door on a person who is rude to me. I've had lost people spit on me, curse me, and even push me off their porches. I didn't have good thoughts about them, but I didn't let them know that. I knew there was going to be a day when they might need me to help them love my God. We must leave the door open.

My father had a friend who was an "Independent" Baptist preacher. He was a capital-"I" independent. He was independent of everything. He was against everything. He was a negative guy. He wouldn't marry a couple unless they had been absolutely 100 percent pure all their lives. They couldn't have even eaten pork 'n beans. He had all kinds of silly rules. I remember one time a couple came to him to be married. They were members of his church, and he asked, "You are members of this church, aren't you? However, I notice you don't come on Sunday nights."

They replied, "No, we don't come on Sunday night."

He retorted, "Well, let Ed Sullivan marry you." He actually said that!

In a real sense, that's what Elisha was saying. "You've been serving this other god—just go ahead and let him take care of your problems." But I still believe that in the matter of witnessing, we need to be at such a point that even when people are rude to us, we act in the Spirit of Christ and leave the door open for a later witness. We must do this.

I want you to notice another truth about this passage. Israel was going to dig the ditches and wait for the water. But look at what happened. The abundant supply came. In verse 20 we read, "And it came to pass in the morning, when the meat offering was offered, that, behold, there came water by the way of Edom, and the country was filled with water." God did what he said he was going to do. God kept his promise.

I like to hear stories about our church. Once when we were visiting, a man told us that there was a time in the life of the church that people mortgaged their homes in order to see First Southern of Del City go forward. That's digging ditches in the valley for God to bring a blessing. I'm convinced the people of our church would do it again if it were necessary. In fact, if we are not willing to go to bigger and better things for God, he will quit blessing us. We must have that kind of spirit. Just because we have 3,000 people in church does not mean that is all God wants us to have. He may want us to have 6,000. We must keep digging the ditches. We can do that by being kind to people we witness to; by waiting for the water to come and expecting the blessings to be abundant.

I was reading recently about the time engineers were trying to build a bridge across New York Harbor. They couldn't find a foundation for one of the buttresses. As they were going under the water with divers, they noticed an old scow that had been buried in bricks and garbage. They needed to put part of the foundation there, but they couldn't because of the old scow. No one could lift it.

They tried every way in the world to remove that way. Finally a young engineer said, "I know how you can move it. Just give me the chance." The others agreed. Well, when the tide was low, he came with a barge that wasn't very big, but on the two wooden piers of the barge, he tied huge ropes. At low tide, he sent the divers down with anchors and they hooked them around that old, heavy scow. The others asked, "Now, what are you going to do?" He said, "I'm not going to do anything. I'm just going to wait." It wasn't long until the tide came up, and the little barge began to lift on the water. The two anchors began to pull and pull, and that old scow was pulled absolutely clear by the power of the rising tide. What moved all that? The power of the Atlantic Ocean.

People, we must be willing to get the power of God behind every effort we undertake. All our ingenuity and all our craftiness will not achieve anything. At some low tides, we need to tie on the anchors and let the power of God's rising tide move the obstacles. Then we can do marvelous things.

Let's notice another thought in verse 15. "Now bring me a minstrel. And it came to pass, when the minstrel played, that the hand of the Lord came upon him." We ought to read through 1 Samuel sometime. Saul needed David to play music for him before he could have any peace. Two of the good things about our churches are the Spirit-filled music and the dedicated music leaders.

I recently read a quote from Martin Luther. He wrote, "One of the finest and noblest gifts of God is music. This is very hateful to the devil, and with it we may drive off temptations and evil thoughts. After theology, I give the next and highest place to music. It has often aroused and moved me so that I have been filled with desire to preach. We ought not to ordain young men to the office of preacher if they have not trained themselves and practiced singing in the school." I'm glad I didn't have to practice singing to to be a preacher. I would have been somewhere else, but I think there is a tremendous truth in this. A couple told me just the other day, "Brother Bailey, one of the reasons we joined First Southern is because the music lifted us to God."

Elisha wouldn't make a decision for God until the minstrel came and played for him. He wanted a minstrel. We ought to keep our singing Christ-honoring, gospel-bound, and centered in the will and purpose of God.

Friends, verse 18 puts me on shouting ground. Look at it! "This is but a light thing in the sight of the Lord." This wasn't even a challenge for God. All he did was a miracle, and that's what God is in the business of doing! Miracles! Don't you know God laughs at some of our prayers. "Oh, Lord, we hope twenty-five people will be saved." Why not 2,500? He said, "I'll bring water without rain; I'll fill your ditches without water coming from the sky, and supply your armies with water. That is but a slight thing for me to do."

Notice what Elisha says in the last part, "He will

deliver the Moabites also into your hand." Do you know what this is saying? When we begin digging ditches around our churches and start doing things we really don't have to do, but we do them in anticipation of the promises God is going to fulfill; when we begin acting in faith instead of merely counting the reasons we are doing things, not only will God bless us, he'll defeat our enemies. God will say, "Not only will I bless you and make you a bigger church and a brighter church and a more Spirit-filled church, but I'm going to 'sock it' to the devil."

Read verses 21-25, and you will discover that he did exactly that. I want us to notice the last phrase of that chapter. After they fought that Moabite king, "they departed from him and returned to their own land" (v. 27). Brother, the devil's crowd gave up. They threw in the towel. We must start acting in faith and digging ditches, and making our music glorify God. People will begin asking for the prophet of God, and God's water will begin to come, and the wells and ditches will be filled. When God's power is abundant, and the Holy Ghost is so warm that people can't help being saved, and Christians can't help being warm, and lives can't help being changed, then we're going to see the devil defeated time and time again.

Not only will God bless, but he's going to say to our churches, "Your blessings of a good-sized church, and people being saved, and great programs are nothing. Just look around, and you're going to see some of the strongholds of the devil break down in the midst of how I am blessing." It is going to happen. The principle is biblical.

I'm ready to dig ditches. How about you? I'm ready to be the prophet God wants me to be. How about you? I am ready to continue to sing music that is Spirit filled and see people who want to join the church because the music speaks to them. How about you? I am ready to see God bless abundantly when all this happens. You can be sure God is going to bless. I'm ready to so extend myself that it's going to take a miracle for God to empower me to do what I've promised him I'll do. If we've only promised God what we ourselves can handle, we have fallen far short of faith. It is when we commit ourselves to more than we can do that we give God room enough to take control. I wonder how many there are who have been afraid to dig ditches. I am telling you that if every one of us could grasp what this passage has to say, it would be all we need to change our churches and turn our areas upside down for Christ.

Dig ditches and stand back and wait. God's promise is about to give us an overflowing blessing.

10
Fighting to Die

There have been many tragedies in history. Certainly, the Civil War was a tragedy. There were 469,000 casualties. And, of course, World War I had 3,000,000. Still, even more tragic was World War II with 250,000 US casualties. What an unbelievable world we live in. There has been tragedy after tragedy.

There was the *Hindenburg,* the huge German zeppelin which exploded and fell, killing many people. There was the sinking of the *Titanic,* horrendous earthquakes, and disastrous hurricanes and tornados. These are unspeakably dreadful tragedies.

Time and again we have been faced with front-page news stories of tragic experiences. But I am going to tell you a much more tragic story than any of these. This tragedy is worse than all of the tragedies of the world accumulated into one. "What is it?" you ask.

It is this—people are fighting to their deaths. They are endeavoring to die. They are making every effort possible to obtain the privilege of dying. They evidently desire death. There are untold millions across this world who are refusing the very thing that will give them life. Apparently, their greatest desire is to die.

Now, most of the time preachers are on the side of the saints. I think that is unfair. I think a preacher should occasionally be on the side of sinners. Thus, I am going to switch sides in this chapter and show those who are determined to die, determined to spend eternity in hell, determined to be without God, how to accomplish their desires. If there is someone who desires to go to hell, I will elaborate what he is going to have to fight.

The Church of Jesus Christ

The first thing you are going to have to fight is the church of Jesus Christ.

The Bible says in 2 Peter 3:9, "The Lord is not slack concerning his promise, as some men count slackness; but is longsuffering to us-ward, not willing that any should perish, but that all should come to repentance."

If this verse expresses the Lord's desire, then it means that he has provided a way for every man, woman, and child on this earth to be saved—to have eternal life. Apparently, some do not want life—they prefer death. In order to die, they will have to fight.

I know of people who have to fight to save their lives, but there are untold millions across the world who are fighting in order to die. You ask, "Why do you have to fight to die eternally?" You must fight the church. The church stands in a sinner's path of going to an eternal hell. Someone says, "Now, Brother Bailey, I know better than that. There are churches all over the world that don't really preach about people being saved or being born again." Yes, but the true church of Jesus Christ has as its greatest emphasis, "Ye must be born again" (John 3:7). The one thing that the true church has to offer above everything else is the saving power of Jesus Christ.

I once preached a revival in California and the pastor took me to a place where they dry-dock ships. Many are in mothballs today. Years ago on board one of those ships was an enormous amount of TNT. It exploded, and a little church near the area was severely damaged.

Everything was lost, except the front wall. The amazing part about it was—it was the front wall which faced the explosion. The whole back of the church was destroyed. It looked as if some mammoth giant had taken it in his hands and made sawdust of it. Nevertheless, the entire front of the church stood. To top that, on the front of that church was a neon sign which flashed the words, "Jesus Saves."

My friend, if there is anything in the world that will stand when everything else has failed, it is the truth that "Jesus saves." If a church is based on that foundation, it will last.

The church of Jesus Christ tells the sinner that he must do away with the church's influence in order to be lost. In order for a sinner to die and go to hell, he will have to fight the powerful influence of the true church of the Savior. If one lets the influence of the church remain, salvation will reside in its very midst. Why? Christ established the church. Some people criticize the church, but, more than likely they will not want to live where there is no church.

A magazine once published an interesting story about a development organization that established a great community center near Las Vegas, Nevada. It was a beautiful place. It had a golf course, swimming pools, and a gorgeous country club. It contained shopping centers, beautiful condominiums, and spacious subdivisions. The lawns and landscaping surrounding the homes were completed, but they weren't selling. The development was everything anyone could desire, but it wasn't selling. Finally, the developers gathered to discuss the problem. They asked, "What are we going to do?" They racked their brains. They tried to analyze why they could not sell the homes. Finally one executive said, "We need a church!" The others replied, "What do you mean? We don't even go to church." He answered, "I know it, but we've got to put a church out there. If we would get us a church and find us a preacher, we could sell every lot."

So, they built a church and brought in a preacher. Sure enough, in a short time every house but two in that development had been sold.

Even people who don't go to church don't want to live in a place that's so pagan that God is not there in some tangible representation. Yes, if the sinner is going to die and spend eternity in hell, he will have to say that every church in this world that preaches the saving power of Jesus Christ is useless and worthless and has no effect on the world. Why? Because the church proclaims that there is saving power in Jesus Christ.

The sinner can fight against the church, and many have tried. They have beat against the iron doors of God's house until their knuckles of skepticism are bleeding with doubt, and yet, the churches of Jesus still prosper and live on. The churches that have died are those who never talked about Jesus, anyway. If the sinner is going to die and go to hell, he must believe at his core that every church he has ever seen or known anything about is worthless.

Surely you have read the story of the Wycliffe Bible Translators who went to Ecuador as witnesses to the Auca Indians and were killed by those very Indians? The story relates that the widow of one of the martyrs returned at a later time and built a little church. People used to warn the witnesses of the head-hunters. They cautioned, "They will have your heads. The headhunters will kill you." But, praise be to God, a little church was erected in those jungles. There is a steeple pointing the

way to God. People now go there and see the church of
God and remark, "Come on. Come on. I see a church."

Oh, yes, the church of Jesus calls, "Sinner, you must
be born again. You must be saved." Now, if the sinner is
going to die and go to hell, he will have to fight against
the influence and power of the church.

The Person of Jesus Christ

The second thing a sinner will have to fight if he is
persistent in his efforts to die is the person of Christ.
After years of denouncing Jesus Christ, a well-known
atheist said at the time of his death, "I am sorry. I regret
every negative word that I have said about Jesus. I have
criticized him and his followers. But I am sorry for every
word that I said about him."

When Jesus Christ died upon the cross, he was saying
to everyone, "I did this so you would not have to die. I
died so you could have life eternal." If a sinner desires to
die, he will have to take the person of Jesus, cast him
down, and denounce him as a fake and a fraud. If one
really wants to die, he must say, in essence, "Jesus, I
want nothing to do with you." You see, Jesus must be
proven worthless. If this is truly done by the sinner, he
will have done something no one else in the world has
ever done.

Can a person really fight successfully against Jesus
and thereby die and spend eternity in hell? Jesus is
extremely powerful. He is wonderful. He is precious. To
the artist, he is the one who is altogether lovely. To the
architect, he is the chief cornerstone. To the builder, he
is the sure foundation. To the baker, he is the living
Bread. To the gardener, he is the rose of Sharon and lily
of the valley. To the carpenter, he is the door of life. To
the geologist, he is the rock of ages. To the jurist, he is

the righteous judge. To the sinner, he is the Lamb of God that taketh away the sin of the world. To the saved, he is the King, the Lord, and the coming Savior. This is the Jesus you must fight against in order to die.

I talked to Colonel Jim Irwin who walked on the moon during Apollo 15. I said, "Jim, why are so many men at NASA Christians?" He looked at me and answered, "Bailey, I think the reason is that we couldn't face what we have to face without Jesus." Isn't that amazing? The Man Who wore sandals and rode a donkey is still the answer. Even for those who go to the moon in a space capsule, he is still the answer. However intelligent we become, if we have a thousand Ph.D.s, without Jesus, man is lost. One can never outgrow Jesus. One can never become too smart for Christ. He is still the Way, the Truth, and the Life, and no man can come to the Father except through him. Jesus is *the answer!*

Years ago a wealthy man died without a will. He had no relatives, so everything he had was auctioned off, including his spacious mansion. After everything else was sold, one elderly lady bought a small picture of a boy. When she took it home, she found an envelope on the back of it. It contained a note which read, "To the one who finds this envelope, take it to an attorney." She carried it to an attorney and discovered that this man had left all his wealth and his entire fortune to the one who bought that little picture. The picture happened to be of the man's only son who had been killed in the war. He had died for his country. He had fought, bled, and died on foreign soil. That man had left all of his millions to anyone who cared enough to buy the picture of his son.

My friend, when you accept Jesus Christ and invite him into your life and say, "I want you to be my Lord; I want you to be my Master; Savior, I want you to be my saving power"; everything God has becomes yours. We become joint heirs with Christ.

> Jesus is the sweetest name I know,
> And He's just the same as His lovely name,
> And that's the reason why I love Him so;
> Oh, Jesus is the sweetest name I know.

LELA LONG

In order to die, one must fight against these truths. The sinner will have to sneer, "Jesus, you are a fake and a fraud. I don't want anything to do with you." That is what must happen, if you persist in dying. Some will die and go to hell, apparently because they have succeeded in resisting the love of their wives, the love of their husbands, the love of their friends, the love of their neighbors, and also the love of Jesus Christ.

How can anyone say no to Jesus? He left us the power of his life. Can you really fight Jesus? Can you really summarily dismiss him?

Years ago in the state of Tennessee there was a little stream with a big lump in the path of a crossing. When anyone would come through the crossing in his covered wagon, he would curse because of this big lump. Finally, someone took the lump up, took it to his home, and used it for a doorstop. One day a man who had a degree in geology saw the lump holding the door back. He examined it and discovered that it was pure gold. Quite a surprise, huh?

My friend, some think that Jesus is a stumbling block. They think this because of their ignorance. Some think that he is no more than a prophet or a good man. However, those who have lifted him high in order to examine him are those who have come to discover that Jesus Christ is pure gold! One does not realize his value until one really looks closely.

If you are determined to go to hell, you will have to believe in your heart that Jesus is a fake and a fraud. You must say that he was an absolute idiot, a liar, and a disgrace to humanity.

Your Own Reasonable Thinking

The sinner must also fight his own "good thinking" if he desires to die. I have heard many people remark, "Oh, Christianity is an emotional thing." My friend, it may be emotional in part, but the most reasonable and intelligent thing one can do is to accept Jesus as Savior. One does not have to be a ding-a-ling to be a Christian. A person who accepts Jesus Christ has made the wisest, most intelligent decision that anyone ever makes. It is a reasonable thing to do. It is an intelligent thing for one to give one's life to Christ.

The other day a man was informing me about all the hypocrites in the church. He was drunk and cursing. He was slapping his wife around and using profanity in front of his little children. Of course, he was telling me of the stupid hypocrites in the church and how Christianity makes you all emotional. He was letting me know one does not even have to think straight to be a Christian and yet, in his condition, he was embarrassing all of us. He didn't get that way because he knew Jesus. He got that way because he didn't know Jesus. The most reasonable thing in the world is to know Jesus.

I heard of a demented lady who was given a beautiful wooden box. Inside was one of the greatest diamonds in the world. She threw away the diamond, but she kept the box. Stupid, huh?

The Bible teaches that a person's soul lives forever, but his body dies. The real diamond, then, is the soul. Most of us take this body, which is temporary, and dress it up, feed it, nurture it, and treat it royally. It is the *box,* not the *diamond!* Someday there will be a casket, a bunch of lilies, and mourners who will weep because you have died. Listen! If one knows Jesus, he has not died. He has merely left the body. He has gone on to be with God. Yet the person who does not know Christ is the person who is majoring on the flesh and neglecting the spirit.

I preached a revival in Louisiana one time and we had dinner with an eighteen-year-old girl. Her body was bent over because some inebriated guy in a pickup truck was driving on the wrong side of the road. His truck went out of control and hit her. She was crushed in the accident. She may never marry or have a normal life. Every day she lives, she is in pain. That tragedy would not have occurred if that man had known Jesus.

If a person wants to do something intellectual, he can turn his life over to Jesus. It will make him wiser, stronger, and never an embarrassment to his family. He will never bring shame on his household if he knows Jesus.

If the sinner is going to die and go to hell, he is going to have to stop being reasonable. He will have to stop thinking sensibly.

The Power of the Holy Spirit

The fourth influence the sinner must fight to die is the power of the Holy Spirit. The Bible teaches that the Holy Spirit was given to convict of sin. When a public invitation to receive Christ is given, people feel the wooing of the Holy Spirit. They feel God's call and God's moving in their lives.

You may taunt sarcastically, "Man, I don't see any Spirit." A little boy was flying a kite. A man came by and chided the boy, saying, "Son, what are you doing?" The lad said, "Flying a kite." The man looked up and saw nothing because of low fog. He said, "I see nothing up there. How do you know the kite is still there?" The boy said, "Sir, because I can feel the tug on the string."

When a person is convicted by the Holy Spirit, he will feel the tug. The sinner will feel the tug and he will have to say, "No, no, no." He will have to fight the convicting power of the Holy Spirit in order to die and go to hell.

The unpardonable sin is when a person blasphemes the Holy Spirit. The work of the Holy Spirit is to convict a person to be saved. If one continues to say no, some day the Holy Spirit will say, "You have had long enough to be saved." Please do not fight what would give you eternal life. Yield and be saved—now!

11
Future Events —
Five Future Facts

This is a time in Christian history when there is a great emphasis placed on prophecy and its connection with future things. This is so because there are so many things that seem to be pointing toward the imminent return of our Lord.

I recently preached a message that indicated how much the energy crisis has caused the current dilemma. There is little doubt that the U.S. would intervene if the Persian Gulf nations should be threatened by the Soviets. If any OPEC country were to be taken by the Communists, America would become excited. Nations have gone to war for much less.

Forty percent of American oil comes from outside sources. Every time we fill our automobiles with gas, we are probably helping to finance the battle of Armageddon. It is entirely possible the end times will highly involve petroleum. We simply cannot do without fuel. We must understand that everything which seems to be taking place now points to the soon return of our Lord. I constantly caution people not to question the fact that Jesus is going to come back to this earth.

We have in our home a small and inexpensive movie projector. As I rewind the films after use, the frames start slowly. But, when I get near the end of the roll, it goes faster and faster until the last frame rips off the reel and the process is complete.

That's the way Bible prophecy seems to be taking

place since the time of Christ. It has moved slowly until
the 50s, 60s and 70s, and now into the 80s. The wheel of
prophecy is turning so rapidly that very soon the last
frame will fly off, and the end of time will have come.
The future is upon us. Much of what has been prophesied in the Scripture has come to pass, and we are now
coming to the final stages. So, let's look closely at five
future facts.

The Rapture of the Church

The first fact in biblical prophecy is the event called
the rapture. The word *rapture* per se is not in the Bible.
It is a later term. It is a Latin word which has reference
to ecstatic relief. It means to be caught up in excitement.
Theologians through the years have taken the word rapture from the Latin derivation and applied it to the ap-
pearing of the Son of God in the sky. The term is not in
the Bible. Rather it is the word that describes the ap-
pearing of Jesus Christ.

The nature of the rapture is that it shall be sudden. It
shall be without warning and shall be final. I remember
hearing Robert Kennedy interviewed after President
John F. Kennedy had been assassinated in Dallas,
Texas. He reported, "You know, Jack almost didn't go
to Dallas. He thought it wasn't the thing to do, but some
of his advisers said that he ought to go ahead and appear
in Dallas." Then I remember Robert Kennedy putting
his hand to his head and saying, "If Jack had it to do
over, he certainly would not have made that trip to
Dallas."

When the rapture comes, every person is going to
realize that they should have been a Christian. When the
rapture comes, they will know they should have accepted Christ. Just as death is final—and just as Presi-

dent Kennedy could not take back that trip to Dallas—
when Jesus Christ comes, it will be a final event. Those
who will be left, will be left. Those who tried to find
"higher" religions such as Buddhism or Hinduism will be
left. Those who have tried to find Muhammad as the
source of their faith and the path to eternal life will be
left upon this earth. No one will go to be with the Lord
Jesus who does not know Him. The rapture will be
sudden. It will be without warning. It will be final.
There will be no time for anyone to write to loved ones.
There will be no time to say farewell to family and
friends. It will be sudden and without warning. The
Bible says it will be as a thief in the night.

Let's examine the biblical doctrine of the rapture.
Notice the passage in 1 Thessalonians 4:13. The Bible
speaks of that glorious day of the rapture of the saints.

The other night when my wife and I were coming back
from a meeting, we looked over in the eastern sky and
saw a beautiful, brilliant light. I could just visualize the
coming of Christ in the framework of the light that
illuminated that part of the sky. I thought to myself,
*Wouldn't it be great if Christ would come? Wouldn't it be
great if indeed Jesus were in the sky? We wouldn't have
to raise the budget. I wouldn't have to prepare a sermon
on the rapture. The rapture would be taking place.
Wouldn't that be a beautiful thing?*

"The day of the Lord so cometh as a thief in the night"
(1 Thess. 5:2). He will come secretly and without warning. It was marvelous when Jesus said, "Come unto me,
all ye that labour and are heavy laden" (Matt. 11:28). It
was glorious when Jesus said, "It is finished" (John
19:30). It was incomprehensible when Jesus said, "Into
thy hands I commend my spirit" (Luke 23:46). It was
almost unbelievable when he said, "He that hath seen

me hath seen the Father" (John 14:9). But, of all the statements that Jesus Christ uttered while he was upon this earth, none is as significant as his return.

The Bible says he will come with a shout! There is no revelation that tells us what Jesus is going to shout when he returns. But I have an idea that he is going to shout to all who have been saved, "I have come. I have come!"

Of course, if you have not been saved, you don't have to worry about what Jesus is going to shout, because you won't hear it. Paul said in 1 Thessalonians 5:2, "The day of the Lord so cometh as a thief in the night." But to whom does this refer? The lost! Only to the lost will he come as a thief in the night. Paul tells us that believers shall hear the trump of God. We shall hear the voice of the archangel. We shall hear the "shout" of Jesus when he comes back. So, please do not think the Bible is contradicting itself when it says, he's coming as a thief, but is going to blow a horn at the same time. You see, the lost won't hear the trumpet. The lost won't hear the voice of the archangel. They will not know when Jesus shouts. We, however, shall not be overtaken as by a thief.

Before the rapture occurs, there will be a man who will be involved in some very obvious activity. His name will be Antichrist. It is possible that at this very hour Antichrist is alive on the earth. He could be laying the groundwork to become a great leader of the European nations. As you realize, when the church is raptured, the restraint of the Holy Spirit will be removed. After the church is gone and the Holy Spirit is gone, the Antichrist will begin to make his rule more attractive. He will make a covenant with Israel for three and one-half years, and he will be a brilliant leader for them. He will establish himself as *the* world leader. One can already hear the television commentators talking about the need for a man of peace. There is a need, they affirm, for a man who can take the splintered areas of society and regiment them and bring them together.

This great leader will see that there is a pressing need for a central religion. During the time of the Antichrist, there will be a dearth of religion. There will be all kinds of difficulties. So, he will establish a religious leader. The Bible calls this religious leader the "false prophet."

Now Antichrist will establish the false prophet and will make a huge statue of him like was made to Nebuchadnezzar. Everyone who falls down and worships the statue will be marked with a special insignia, and it will be representative of the false prophet. They will be marked on the back of their hand, or upon their forehead with the mark, "666." Six is the number of man. Seven is the number of perfection. Seven is the number of God. It is the number of completion. Man always falls short of seven, of course, and therefore six to the third power form the "unholy trinity." As the Father, Son, and the Holy Spirit are the Holy Trinity, so the Antichrist, the false prophet, and the dragon is the unholy trinity— "666." Man to the third power.

Revelation 14:9-11 says that when the Antichrist begins his work, there will be the opportunity to worship the false prophet who is a part of a great world empire and a great world church. The book of Revelation calls that church "the harlot." When you find the word *harlot* in the book of Revelation, it refers to the false prophet's church or religion.

In review, let's put two and two together. This religious leader could be prominent in our day. He will be revered as the greatest religious leader on the face of the earth. The people who fall down and worship him will receive "the mark of the beast." They will be the only ones who will be able to buy food. Others will go into grocery stores and the management will say, "Stick your hand under the machine." If there is no "666" mark, they will not be able to buy food. The ones who have the mark will be the only ones who will be able to hold jobs. They will be the only ones who will be able to borrow at the bank.

Imagine the temptation for everyone on earth to bow before the beast and say, "Yes, mark my hand. Mark my head. I want the '666.' " However, as we read the Scripture, it says that everyone who has the mark shall be cast into the lake of burning fire and brimstone, and the smoke of their torment shall ascend unto the nostrils of God.

Listen! The very things that the world will have to choose between then, people must choose between now. There are some who have taken the mark of the beast now. People have said, "Look at all of the advantages." Young men and women have lost their purity in illicit relationships in order to have the approval of society. For example, some girls have taken off their clothes and posed for men's magazines in order to have the approval of the "beast." Wonder of wonders, some preachers have said, "That's just fine!" Friends, those preachers are false prophets.

Some have taken the mark of the beast on their lives instead of the purity and protection of Jesus. They think it is fine and cool and smart. But the Bible says that if people take the mark of the beast and all of his advantages, one day they will be cast into fire and brimstone. The same choice the world will be forced to make, after those who are saved are raptured, is the choice they must make now. It is the choice of that which is "Antichrist" or "for Jesus." Which is it going to be?

Look at Matthew 24:36-40. Jesus is going to come. It will be a day like the days of Noah. They will be living life similar to that on any given Saturday. Imagine a guy shining his Mark V, living in his $150,000 home. When I ask him to attend church, he doesn't curse me or curse God. He just doesn't give "a flip." He's got his beer, his chips and dips, and he's stuffing his gut. His stomach is hanging out over his belt as he's washing his car. He's living it up. His son is in the yard using the $500 mower. Afterwards, they go into the air-conditioned home and turn on the color TV. They're just living it up. America has not cursed God! America has forgotten God! People are just eating and drinking and forgetting God.

As it was in the day of Noah, so shall it be in the day of the coming of the Son of man. But remember, they were left out of the ark, and so will those who have forgotten God now be left outside of Jesus Christ. The rapture is fact number one, and it shall come without any warning. No one can be with Christ unless he has been saved.

The Judgment Seat of Christ

Look at 1 Corinthians 4:5, as we discuss the second future fact. Other references are found in Romans 14:10 and 1 Corinthians 3:10-15.

The Bible teaches that after the rapture occurs, we shall stand at the judgment seat of Christ. Everyone who stands at the judgment seat of Christ, however, will be going to heaven. The judgment seat of Christ is only for the saved. The lost people will not be there. The self-righteous, agnostic people will not be there. Only those who are saved will be there. The word *judgment* is a Greek word, *bema*. The *bema* was a part of the Greek arena. What was the "bema"? In the vast arena where the Olympic games were played there was one elevated seat. On that elevated seat sat the king. The king would look down on those who performed in the arena. As he watched, if he pointed his thumb up, the participants were all right. But, if he pointed his thumb down, they soon lost their heads! The king passed judgment. He was the "bema." He was the judge of the events.

Another part of the Olympic games was the king's giving rewards. There would be wonderful, glorious rewards given. The participants would come up and kneel before the "bema." They would look up to the oval box where the king sat. His judgment would also fall on those who had run a good race.

In the day when Christians stand before the "bema" of Christ, he will judge us on how well we did at living the Christian life. Christ himself will judge us. The Bible declares that he will judge the hidden things of darkness. He will judge the counsels of the heart. God's tape recorder has been on as we live our lives. God's holy stenographer has taken every note that we have spoken, every word that we have ever uttered. God has transcribed it and one day we will stand before the "bema," the judgment seat of Christ.

Immediately after we have been raptured, we will be judged according to our works. The Bible teaches that in that day we will be given five crowns.

One will be the crown of life. This crown is given to those who have been martyred. It is given to those who have died for the cause of Christ. Christian history records that, during the Roman rule, young Christian men and women would be marched into the arena and would have to face the emperor. He would ask them, "You, do you call yourself a Christian?" "Yes! Yes, I do."

The emperor would command for the young person to be stripped. Afterwards, all of the people in the arena would make fun of that person's nakedness. The emperor would then say, "How about it now? Are you still a follower of that fake, Jesus Christ?" "Yes, I am, sir," the Christian youth would testify. The emperor would become enraged and command, "Say, 'Caesar is Lord.'" The young person would say, "No! Christ is Lord." Then they would take that Christian youth, strap him/her to the horns of a bull, and let the bull run into the arena. At the other end of the arena they'd open a trap door, and out would come a half dozen lions that had not been fed for two weeks. The hungry lions would want to feed upon the bull, and as they would fight the bull, they'd tear the young person's body to bits. The only thing the youth would have had to do was look up to the emperor and shout, "Caesar is Lord!" But, as the youth was being torn apart, she/he would cry, "Jesus Christ is Lord."

Since this is actual history, we can easily see that Christians today are a bunch of softies. We don't know what sacrifice is. We have disgraced Almighty God. We have walked upon the blood of those who loved Jesus more than we will ever love him. For the people who died like that, the Bible teaches that at the judgment seat of Christ they will be given a crown of life.

Then the Bible speaks of the crown of righteousness. This will go to those who look forward to the second coming of Christ. The third crown is called the crown of rejoicing. This will go to those who have been soul-winners. The Bible also speaks of the crown of glory that will go to pastors. Then, there is the crown incorruptible that will go to those who have kept their lives pure and above reproach. After receiving the crowns, we'll remove them from our heads and we'll place them at his feet. Then we will sing, "King of kings and Lord of lords!" There is going to be the judgment seat of Christ. This is the second future fact.

The Great Tribulation

The third future fact is called the great tribulation. In Matthew 24:21-23 our Lord speaks about the great tribulation. There is so much involved in this passage that we will certainly have no space to deal with it adequately. However, in a brief synthesis, when the rapture takes place, we Christians will stand before the judgment seat of Christ. For the people who are left on the earth after the rapture, there will be the great tribulation. The first three and one-half years is called the tribulation. But, Jesus referred to the last three and one-half years of life upon this earth as the "great tribulation."

In the book of Daniel, the seventy weeks are the key to a study of prophecy. One cannot study prophecy unless he is familiar with the book of Daniel and his seventy weeks. With this in mind, we also note that Leviticus 25 and other passages refer to weeks not only as seven days, but seven years. In other words, seven years can also mean a week. This is similar to the word *dozen*. One can say, "Bring me a dozen." "A dozen what?" "Never mind what! Just bring me a dozen." Now, when you read of the week in the Bible, it is very much like the word *dozen*. You can have a dozen doughnuts, a dozen eggs, or a dozen apples. You can also have a week of days, a week of weeks, a week of months, or a week of years.

Daniel told us, in an amazing prophecy, that there will be seventy weeks of years. Seventy times seventy is 490 years. And in Daniel 9, the prophet said it will be the time from the beginning of when the Jews return to Israel and the cutting off of the Messiah.

Robert Anderson, a brilliant English lawyer, calculated some interesting facts surrounding the 490-year period about which Daniel prophesied. For example, from the time that Nehemiah took the children of Israel from Babylonian captivity back to Jerusalem by the decree of King Artaxerxes until the time of the coming of Christ and the crucifixion of Christ (which was the "cutting off" of the Messiah) was 483 years. Now, 483 years from 490 years leaves seven years. This means that all of the prophecy of Daniel 9 has been fulfilled except for *seven years*.

You say, "What happened?" Well, when the Jews rejected Jesus Christ, it stopped the time clock of Jewish philosophy, Jewish history, and Jewish prophecy. God will have a special work for his people, the Jews. This is the point at which Gentile prophecy began to take place. John said of Jesus, "He came unto his own, and his own received him not" (John 1:11). So, the Gentile prophecy began at the death of Christ where the Jewish prophecy stopped. All right, the Gentile prophecy will stop at the point of the rapture of the church, and the Jewish prophecy will begin again. In other words, the rapture will be the beginning of the seven years that remain from Daniel's prophecy. These will be the years of the "great tribulation." These years will not begin until you and I are taken up to be with Christ.

During the last seven years, the Antichrist will make an agreement for the first three and one-half years with Israel. They will love him. But, at the end of that three and one-half years, he will turn against the Jewish people. His reason may well be his need of support from Arabs and oil in order to fight his war which will be the battle of Armageddon. This is the last and great war in which the Antichrist takes a ten-member league of nations to battle against the forces of the king of the north (Russia) and the king of the east (China) at the conclusion of the second three and one-half years.

Remember, you and I will come with Jesus Christ from glory to the battle of Armageddon site, and we will defeat the Antichrist. Also, remember that during the time of the great tribulation, there will be hailstones that will fall from the sky weighing 100 pounds each. There will be fire literally running across the earth. The Bible speaks of scorpions as big as men that will move across the earth stinging those who have not given their lives to Christ. Monstrous horrors will happen during the final plagues of the great tribulation for those who have been left. I think you should plan to miss the tribulation. What do you say? Be saved now!

The Reign of Christ upon the Earth

The fourth future fact is the glorious reign of our Lord Jesus Christ upon this very earth.

What's going to happen when the battle of Armageddon is concluded? Jesus is going to defeat Antichrist and deliver him a knockout blow. We are going to be rid of the devil who will ultimately be placed in chains and cast into the pit. But following the battle of Armageddon, *we* (Christians) are going to rule this earth for 1,000 years. One day, those of us who have been saved will be the ambassadors for Christ for a thousand years. You question, "Preacher, I don't understand why Jesus is going to rule and reign upon this earth for a thousand years." There are two reasons, the first being he will do it to show all men what they could have had if they had not turned him down.

You see, during those 1,000 years, a little child will be able to take an asp off a tree and play with it. A lion and a lamb will lie down together, play together, and eat together. Disease will be unheard of. There will never be any sneezing or coughing. Oh! It will be a glorious time of perfect peace upon this earth, according to the Bible.

The second reason will be to show man that circumstances will not bring Utopia, because during the millennium, while we are reigning upon this earth, those who don't know Christ will have some of the most miserable experiences the world has ever known. Man is going to see that, even though his circumstances are perfect, there will still be millions of people who are lost upon this earth and are having unbelievable problems. Why? They have said no so long to the things of righteousness that they will not even be able to think straight enough to say yes and yield.

The Great White Throne Judgment

The fifth and final fact is the awesome great white throne judgment. We find this recorded in Revelation 20:11-15.

Who will be at the great white throne judgment? Here they are! The self-righteous people. For example, the Baptists who were never saved. The Nazarenes who were never saved. The Pentecostals who were never saved. Then, there will be the agnostics, the haughty people, the arrogant people, the guy who slammed the door in the faces of those who come to share Jesus, the fellow who put the sign on his door that says, "No Solicitors, Peddlers, Salesmen, or Preachers."

My friend, these will be at the great white throne judgment. Now listen, they will not be judged as to whether they will go to hell. If they stand at the great white throne judgment, they *will* go to hell. The only reason they will be judged is according to the degree of their punishment. The Bible says, "according to their works" (v. 13). People who go to hell from Washington, D.C., will have it a lot hotter than those to go to hell from Africa. Those who know and have mocked, ridiculed, and rejected the gospel will have it much hotter than those from India or Africa or another place where the gospel is not proclaimed.

The Bible says they will all stand before the great white throne judgment of God and be sentenced to be locked up forever in the madhouse of the universe called hell. John 12:48 teaches that the judge will be the Son. The judge is going to be Jesus. The Bible also says that those who answer no to God's invitation will hear the very words of the gospel on the day of judgment. The very words that they rejected will one day be heard again—but they won't be able to respond. They will cry, "It's too late."

Be careful. The living God of heaven will pass judgment on those who refuse his great salvation. If you will receive Jesus Christ as personal Savior right now, he will receive you, and you will never have to face him as judge. Know him as Lord and master and be saved from his inevitable wrath. He loves you!

12
Be Awake

When we are caught up in a great worship service, we sometimes think the whole world is "Christian" and excited about what is going on inside the church. But the heartbreaking truth is: it just isn't so. In fact, when we look at the priorities God has given us, we discover that the job is being done pitifully and poorly.

Churches seem to be growing in numbers, at least in "casual memberships." It seems that in some ways many churches have had at least some kind of nominal success. But in really making disciples, it seems that we have not done what God wants us to do. Only one third of this world claims to even know Jesus Christ. One third of this world says yes to Jesus Christ, but two thirds say no. If we keep winning people to Christ at the same rate as we now do, in my lifetime alone only one percent of this world will be Christian! We need to mentally chew on that for a moment! It's tragic that my children and grandchildren will live most of their lives in a world that is 99 percent against Jesus Christ.

We have sorely and bitterly failed at our God-given task of winning the world. Some have claimed that the church is washed up and through. One man wrote a stinging poetic accusation against the church when he said, "Outwardly splendid as of old, inwardly sparkless, void, and cold. Her force and fire all spent and gone, like the dead moon, she still shines on."

He is writing that the church is nothing but a reflec-

tion of the past, something that others with more dedicated stamina did years before us, and we are merely
the recipients of their greater and more worthy dedication.

We have beautiful churches, well-appointed buildings
which are heated in the winter and air-conditioned in the
summer, stained-glass windows, and comfortable, cush-
ioned pews.

We have been able to have a "better" life and more
comfort, and yet it is surprising to me that, even though
churches have larger budgets and prettier buildings, it
is costing more than ever to win a person to Christ. It is
pathetic that the very work God told us to do and Jesus
commissioned us to do is what we are absolutely not
doing.

When we look at all the church has done, and yet it
continues to fail in discipling people, I think that we
probably remind the Lord of the little boy who brought
home his report card with an "F" in English, an "F" in
spelling, an "F" in arithmetic, and an "F" in writing, but
an "A" in deportment and citizenship. The daddy took
the report card, looked at it, and then at his son, re-
marking, "Son, it looks like you are a neat, well-man-
nered, *stupid* kid."

Today the church of Jesus Christ is making A's in
everything that doesn't matter. We are making A's in
most everything that is peripheral, but in the *main* thing
he has told us to do, we are making an "F." The church is
flunking in the business of winning people to Christ,
while in the matter of other concerns that are not as
important, we are really flourishing. The answer is that
we must be awake and alert!

When the *Titanic* was going down in the icy waters of
the Atlantic, it radioed a signal to a nearby ship. The

radio operator of the other vessel had just taken off the earphones, wrapped them around his neck, and had gone fast asleep. Even though the SOS signal was coming into those speakers, the man did not hear it because he was sound asleep. God is calling the churches of today to be awake and alert. If we are not, we are going to miss what God has told us to do.

One president of the U. S. supposedly said, "I will either be your best president, or I will be your last." We know he wasn't the last president, and it is a matter of political judgment whether he was the best. We may be the best Christians who have ever lived, or we may well be the last. The forces of Satan are so strong across our world that every year there is a smaller percentage of Christians than the year before.

Each year, on an average, all the people of the Southern Baptist Convention win only the number of people born on January 1 and January 2. We reach, percentage-wise, two days out of 365. That does not include the people already living and lost.

In evangelizing the world, we have not done what Jesus commanded us to do in the Great Commission. If we continue to be the kind of Christians we are, and if the churches of America keep being the kind of churches they are, we are sunk and have irrevocably lost the battle that is before us.

In Matthew 26:36-45 we read,

> Then cometh Jesus with them unto a place called Gethsemane, and saith unto the disciples, Sit ye here, while I go and pray yonder. And he took with him Peter and the two sons of Zebedee, and began to be sorrowful and very heavy. Then saith he unto them, My soul is exceeding sorrowful, even unto death: tarry ye here, and watch with me. And he went a little farther, and fell on his face, and prayed, saying, O my Father,

if it be possible, let this cup pass from me: nevertheless not as I will, but as thou wilt. And he cometh unto the disciples, and findeth them asleep, and saith unto Peter, What, could ye not watch with me one hour? Watch and pray, that ye enter not into temptation: the spirit indeed is willing, but the flesh is weak. He went away again the second time, and prayed, saying, O my Father, if this cup may not pass away from me, except I drink it, thy will be done. And he came and found them asleep again: for their eyes were heavy. And he left them, and went away again, and prayed the third time, saying the same words. Then cometh he to his disciples, and saith unto them, Sleep on now, and take your rest: behold, the hour is at hand, and the Son of man is betrayed into the hands of sinners.

How can we be awake during these crucial days?

Be Grateful

I think we are going to be awakened when we remember all that we have to be grateful for. These men were not casual, vague, or distant disciples. These were the greatest people God had on earth. No group of people lived anywhere who loved Jesus any more than did these men who went to sleep. These were the finest disciples that Jesus had following him. Most of them had been with him all of the three years of his ministry. They walked, talked, and slept with him.

Jesus said to them, "Could ye not," and he points his finger at those disciples who should have known better than to go to sleep. If Peter, James, and John had been awake as they should have been, they would have remembered all of the good things they had seen Jesus do. Jesus looked at those disciples and said, "Could ye not?" Jesus did not use some kind of nebulous word. He said, "Could ye not watch with me this one hour?"

Who is "Ye?" "YE disciples who have seen me go over

to a blind person and take a little spit and clay and put it on the blind man's eyes. YE desciples saw that man see YE disciples saw that lame man walk. YE disciples saw that woman who was burdened about her child's death. YE saw that child come forth from the dead. YE saw those hungry people and they were fed. YE saw me speak and raise Lazarus from the dead. YE disciples have seen me when the little children pressed in upon me, and I loved them and cared for them. YE saw the compassion and love on my face. YE have seen me walk miles. YE have seen the water turned into wine. YE have seen people who were so despondent raised up. One time you were on the sea and the sea was tempestuous, but YE have seen me still the storm and bring peace to your troubled hearts." Those are the people he was talking to.

When Jesus emphasized that word *YE*, he was saying that above all people on earth, they should have known better than to go to sleep! Today Jesus is saying, "YE have seen homes brought back together. YE have seen the Holy Spirit as a dove come and wave it's softening wings. YE have seen God working in area crusades. YE have seen him through a thousand ministries. YE have seen people fall on their faces, weeping before a holy God, repenting of their sins, getting right with God."

God is saying that he wants us to be awake, alert, and responsive to what he has asked us to do. If we desire to be concerned about souls, and have compassion for the hearts of persons, we must begin to enumerate the blessings of God we have seen in our lives and in our homes and in our churches. James and John forgot to be thankful for awhile. That's why they went to sleep.

Had they remembered how Jesus treated them on one occasion alone, they would have been awake when Jesus asked them to. There was a time when their mother came to Jesus and said, "Jesus, I want my sons to be on your left hand and on your right hand in the kingdom of God." And Jesus said, "You'll need to be servants." Jesus could have turned to her and her sons, and with a bitter rebuttal, cut them verbally to pieces, but he loved them and cared for them.

Every one of us could stand and say, "Jesus, I love you. Jesus, you have intervened in my life when I was trying to ruin it, and you saved me. Jesus, you have blessed me a thousand times over and I thank you for it."

Remember the goodness of God! Remember it! Some of us go to sleep instead of being what God wants us to be. In Arkansas a woman worked in the cotton fields from sunup to sundown in order to send her son through college. The boy went off to college and received his degree, but his mother was broken in pain from years of labor in the boiling sun. After he graduated from college, the boy never once came back to his mother's house to say, "Mother, I love you. I thank you for those years of toil." He never once said, "Mother, thank you for sending me the money instead of spending it on yourself." He forgot the one who had provided for him.

Do we remember how good God has been to us? Some say, "Well, I worked for it!" But who gave us the brain? Who gave us the body? God did! We didn't work for anything! God gave us good jobs and good bodies in order to work and earn, and we ought to know it is all a gift from God.

Jesus uses the term, "Could ye not," but we need to see another emphasis. "Could ye not watch with me one hour?" The word *hour* in Greek does not mean sixty minutes. The phrase can accurately be translated, "Could you not watch with me this one occasion?" Jesus is calling to us today, "Could you not watch with me this one occasion when I need you in such a special way? I need you to be winning people to Christ. I need you to be praying. I need you to be giving. I need you to be alert."

Be Unselfish

The disciples could have stayed awake if they had not been primarily concerned with themselves. I can imagine that James must have said to John, as they were there, "Hey, John, what did Jesus just say?" John said, "He said we ought to stay awake." He looked over, but James was already asleep.

People often do what they want to and then alibi "Jesus will understand." "Watch? We're tired!" they said. There is no law to prevent us from coming to church tired. Jesus required those disciples to give up more than luxury. He told them to do without something everyone needs—sleep. He said, "Could you not be awake with me this one hour?"

They were tired and had been walking all day long. They had sacrificed time and again for the cause of his ministry, and yet Jesus said, "I want you to be willing even to give up sleep in order to watch with me." I don't know many people who would give up a life necessity to follow Jesus. Most of us would give up a luxury if we were really begged to do so, but Jesus even asked those disciples to give up sleep on this occasion in order to be what they ought to have been.

The only way a revival comes is when people are willing to count nothing their own, but to count everything as loss for Jesus' sake. Those disciples began thinking about how tired they were, and they went to sleep.

Every time God speaks to us and we start to think about ourselves, we will go to sleep. Jesus said, "So likewise, whosoever he be of you that forsaketh not all that he hath, he cannot be my disciple" (Luke 14:33). Some alibi, "I have other engagements." Some sidestep, "I have a previous commitment." Every church member should say to the world, "I have a previous commitment. He's called Jesus." He ought to be number one in our hearts and lives.

The year after I graduated from Ouchita Baptist University in Arkadelphia, Arkansas, a young ministerial student, his girl friend, and another couple went out to a place we called Low Water Bridge on the Hot Springs Highway. Just as they were about to climb out of the car, one of the girls said, "Mike, I forgot my purse. I need to go back to the dormitory. I must have it." So, all four of them got back into the little car and went down a gravel road to the Hot Springs Highway. On their way back to Arkadelphia, just as they came over a hill, a pickup truck on the wrong side of the road hit that little car head-on. That young, brilliant ministerial student was the only one hurt in the accident. The other three got out. The steering wheel column had penetrated near his heart and crushed him between it and the seat of the car.

The other boy ran to the highway and began to wave his hand. Finally a lady in a large, expensive automobile stopped and pushed the electric window button.

He said, "Ma'am, if you will look up this gravel road, you will see the back of a pickup truck and just on the other side there is a little Volkswagen. There has been an awful wreck, and a friend of mine is in there, bleeding to death. I believe that if you would come and put him in your car and take him to the Clark County Hospital, his life will be saved. Ma'am, you have just got to help us." As she closed the car window, she said, "Son, I don't want to get involved in anything." And off she went on her way.

That young ministerial student, who probably would have been standing in some church preaching the unsearchable riches of Christ today, pumped his last drops of blood onto the floor of that little car. That negligent woman is no worse than many Baptists. For when the time comes around for a Baptist to teach a class or to become involved, they have the great courage to say, "Well, if you don't find anyone else, let me know." Imagine how many people spend eternity in hell apart from God because some Baptist excuses himself with, "I don't want to get involved."

If we are going to be thinking about ourselves, God can't use us. It is so easy to think about how much *self* needs rather than what *God* needs. Jesus said to those disciples, "Stay awake, be alert, I need you."

During my last year in college, I was pastor of a little church in the delta region of Arkansas. One Friday night I went down for a prayer meeting. On prayer meeting night the women always sat on one side and the men sat on the other side of the church. One night I looked over and saw one of our deacons, but his wife, who was always with him, was not there that particular night. After the service I inquired, "Where's your wife?" He said, "Oh, Brother Bailey, she couldn't come." I asked, "What's wrong?" He said, "I really hate to tell you, but we had picked out a television set up at Lake Village and it had a 21-inch screen. Our screen is only a 17-inch. She has been wanting that bigger television set. So, yesterday we went to pick it up and bring it home, but they had sold it. She is just having a nervous shake-a-part over this. It's just horrible. I need you to go see her."

I said, "I'll be glad to go see her." So I got into my old

'55 Ford and drove down that gravel road, across an old bridge to their house, which was situated a long way off the road. I parked my car, walked up on the front porch, looked through the screen door, and could see all the way through the living room and into the bedroom. There was the lady in bed. I knocked on the door and heard a little, trembling voice respond, "Come in." I went on into the living room, and back to the bedroom, stood at her bedside.

I said, "I'm so sorry about all this."

She said, "Oh, Brother Bailey, it is so horrible. It is so terrible." She looked up to me with tearful eyes and said, "Would you pray?" I had never prayed for a television before, but I prayed something.

I climbed back into my car and returned to that little white-frame parsonage next to that country church and I began to cry. I said, "Lord, here's a lady who has worked as the president of our ladies' missionary organization. Here's a lady who has been so active in the work of the church, but I have never known her to shed a tear for all the people around her neighborhood who are lost and on their way to a devil's hell. But she can weep because she could not increase the size of her television screen by four inches."

Be Obedient

If we are going to be awake when Jesus needs us, we must realize that blessings come to the obedient. Did Jesus want those disciples to be awake because he wanted them to arm themselves with swords and stop the Roman soldiers as they came? No. Was it so they could make some kind of big fuss about his being taken away? No.

I believe with all of my heart that when Jesus said,

"Come up here a little ways," went to the big rock, and placed his hands upon it to pray, he wanted them to be awake because he knew they could hear him talking to the Father. Jesus knew it wouldn't be long until he would ascend to the Father and never see the disciples face to face again in this world. Jesus knew that if those disciples could remember having seen him and having heard him talking with the Father, it would be a compulsion and motivation as they fulfilled the Great Commission. It would have compelled them to be the greatest disciples on the earth.

The Holy Spirit does his work and that's it. Those who missed Pentecost, missed it. It never was repeated. The Holy Spirit can do good and worthwhile things, but if we miss them because we are asleep, we are going to miss what Jesus wants to do in our lives.

When Jesus came back from the grave and appeared to the disciples, Thomas was missing. Thomas is often called "Doubting Thomas." Because he didn't make the meeting, and when they told him they had seen Jesus, he replied, "No, you disciples, you have been at it again. You are just trying to save your skin. Jesus is dead. I saw him on the cross, bleeding. I saw him say to the Father, 'Into thy hands I commend my spirit.' Jesus is dead." They answered, "Thomas, we saw him. Thomas, he was here."

Naaman, the Syrian captain, had white, peeling skin because of leprosy. The prophet of God communicated a message through a little maid. She told him that if he would dip in the Jordan River seven times, he would have the skin of a little child. He could have dipped six times, gotten up, looked at himself, and said, "Man, I knew there wasn't anything to it. I dipped six times in the crooked Jordan River and I am still full of leprosy."

Until he had dipped that other time, he did not have one ounce of improvement. But when he dipped that seventh time and was obedient, God blessed him.

May God help us to be obedient to him and stay awake in his service.

13
The Problem of
Unanswered Prayer

God does not have to fit anyone's concept of who he is. God is who he is, not what we want him to be. If you were to talk to all socioeconomic levels of American society, you would find varied opinions on who God really is.

People seemingly want to carve God out of their own desires into the image of what they want him to be. But God is not what we expect him to be; God is not even what we want him to be; God is not what we desire for him to be; God is not the product of our imaginations; God is God! God can be whoever God wants to be.

Old-time theologians called this capacity the "Sovereignty of God." This means God can do anything he wants to do. He is a sovereign God. He does not have to act because we think it is just, merciful, kind, or loving. God can do whatever he wants to do. That's one reason we know he is God. He doesn't have to answer to any of our logic, intellectual schemes, observations, or twisted reasoning. God is God.

In that regard, there are some prayers in which God is not interested. Sometimes, by humanity's definition, God can be very cruel. To humans God can be very impatient.

Look at Proverbs 28:9, "He that turneth away his ear from hearing the law, even his prayer shall be abomination." Have you ever prayed a prayer that did you harm? God says it is possible. Look in Isaiah 1, "Bring no more

vain oblations; incense is an abomintation unto me."
[God says, "Don't bring your tithes and offerings."] He
says, "The new moons and sabbaths, the calling of as-
semblies [I'm tired of your revival meetings], I cannot
away with; it is iniquity, even the solemn meeting.[Even
when you look holy, it is a sin.] Your new moons and
your appointed feasts my soul hateth: they are a trouble
unto me; I am weary to bear them. And when ye spread
forth your hands, I will hide mine eyes from you: yea,
when ye make many prayers, I will not hear" (Isa.
1:13-15).

According to the above Scriptures, there are times
when God does not hear prayers. I have heard people
say, "Well, God always hears prayers, and he always
answers prayers." I have heard this all of my life—even
from preachers. But God does not always hear prayers.

Some claim God always answers prayer—sometimes
it is yes, sometimes it is no, and sometimes it is wait
awhile. However, in reality, sometimes God doesn't
answer at all. Sometimes he ignores a prayer. Sometimes he hears a prayer that brings abomination on a
man who would pray such a prayer.

As our prayer life goes, so will go the evangelistic response in any church. If we could have evangelistic
meetings without prayer, no one would want the results. If we could report that a thousand people have
made some kind of decision, it would only be "wood, hay,
and stubble"—if it is not the result of God's blessings
upon the effort.

There is much ignorance concerning prayer. I knew of
two men who got together on one occasion. Neither had
been to church often. On this particular day, they had a
little too much to drink.

As they were talking, one of them said, "I'll bet you

are not very religious."

"I'll have you know I'm more religious than you."

"No, I'm more religious."

"No, I'm more religious," said the second man.

The first one said, "I bet you don't even know the Lord's prayer." "Yes, I know it," replied the second.

The first man said, "If you can say the Lord's Prayer, I'll give you five dollars." The second fellow said, "All right. 'Now I lay me down to sleep, I pray the Lord my soul to keep.' "

The first fellow took out his billfold, handed over the five dollars, and said, "I didn't think you could do it." Yes, there's much ignorance concerning prayer.

A man never stands taller than when he is on his knees. A pulpit committee in West Texas called their director of missions and said, "We want you to recommend a preacher to us." In that West Texas church, it seemed that every man was a big, raw-boned, rugged cowpoke. The director of missions asked the head of the pulpit committee, "How big a preacher do you want?" The chairman of the pulpit committee answered, "We really don't care how big he is, but we would like to request that he be the kind of man who, when he gets on his knees, is big enough to reach heaven." That's a big preacher!

What are the prayers God will not answer? What are the prayers that God is not interested in? What are the prayers that could be an abomination to God and a curse upon the one who delivers such prayers? There are at least six.

Prayers About Doubt

First, God will not answer the prayers of doubt. James 1:6-7 says, "But let him ask in faith, nothing wavering. [That is, no unbelief.] For he that wavereth is like a wave of the sea driven with the wind and tossed. For let not that man think [it is that man who is unbelieving, that is wavering] that he shall receive anything of the Lord." A man who is an unbeliever, a skeptic, a doubter, an agnostic, or a man who puts a question mark after the truth of the Bible will never get anything from God.

Churches with pastors who put a question mark over the virgin birth, the second coming, the blood atonement, and the inspiration of the Scriptures—almost never have people born again or changed under their ministry. They rarely have drunkards become sober or have prostitutes turn into virtuous women. The reason is that God is not eager to have sceptics of his holy Word and power.

My mind is made up about the Bible, the Word of God. If that's being narrow-minded, let me say that I'm just as narrow-minded as the Word of God. I've heard of people so narrow-minded they could look through a keyhole with both eyes at the same time. I don't want to be quite *that* narrow-minded, but we need to remember that one can get so broad-minded that he doesn't have a cutting edge. It's only the narrow edge that cuts. To get your prayers answered, you must believe.

Some may ask, "Preacher, do I have to believe in prayer?" No, the Bible does not say you must have faith in prayer. You must have faith in God. We must believe God wants to answer prayer, that God is going to answer prayer, and that what God has to say in his Book is true, because a wavering, skeptical person is not going to get anything from God.

The same thing is true about salvation. The Bible says,"Believe on the Lord Jesus Christ, and thou shalt be saved" (Acts 16:31). Romans 10:9 says, "That if thou shalt confess with thy mouth the Lord Jesus, and shalt believe in thine heart that God hath raised him from the dead, thou shalt be saved." God teaches that when a person is doubtful and doesn't have enough confidence in the almighty, living sovereign, omnipotent, omniscient, omnipresent God to believe that when one prays, one's prayers will be answered, will *not* have prayers answered.

I'm not talking about an occasional honest doubt. Rather, I speak of those who brag and boast that they doubt the Bible, the validity of prayer, the holiness of God's Word. The Bible says that "Without faith it is impossible to please him" (Heb. 11:6).

An example of a lack of power is found in Matthew 17:14-20:

> And when they were come to the multitude, there came to him a certain man, kneeling down to him, and saying, Lord, have mercy on my son: for he is lunatic and sore vexed: for ofttimes he falleth into the fire, and oft into the water. [Maybe the son had seizures of some kind.] And I brought him to thy disciples, and they could not cure him. Then Jesus answered and said, O faithless and perverse generation, how long shall I be with you? [Now he's talking to the disciples.] How long shall I suffer you? bring him hither to me. And Jesus rebuked the devil: and he departed out of him: and the child was cured from that very hour. Then came the disciples of Jesus apart, and said, Why could not we cast him out? And Jesus said unto them, Because of your unbelief: for verily I say unto you, If ye have faith as a grain of mustard seed, ye shall say unto this mountain, Remove hence to yonder place; and it shall remove; and nothing shall be impossible unto to you.

Like the disciples, wouldn't it be sad to pray and yet have no power? These disciples had done all the magic of preparation. They built the platform, had the choir, the PA system, and the media. But, even though they had done everything, people did not get right with God because the disciples had lost their power.

A man in our church put me to shame after services one day. I had been telling about 400 who had been saved in our Starlite Crusade, and he came to me and said, "Preacher, we don't have to keep our average at 400. You wouldn't be mad if 800 were saved, would you?" I said, "Sir, that wouldn't bother me a bit."

If you have a belief problem, or a faith problem, settle it. Invest your life in believing. Put your soul into it. Have faith!

A man once stood before a host of people at Niagara Falls and said, "How many of you believe that I can walk across Niagara Falls on this wire while pushing a wheelbarrow?" All raised their hands, believing he could do it. They wanted to see him do it or fall into Niagara Falls. One man shouted, "I believe you can do it!" The man on the high wire said, "Sir, you come and get in the wheelbarrow, please." The man on the ground said, "No, I believe *you* can do it, but I don't want to be in that wheelbarrow."

Faith is not intellectual assent. Faith is affirming "Jesus Christ, I step across the line of my own self-interest and my own desires. I give myself lock, stock, and barrel to you. I believe your Word with all my heart. God, the matter is settled. I put my trust, faith, and total existence into you." That's faith, and when you pray with that kind of heart, God says he'll hear your prayers.

Prayers of Selfishness

A second prayer God will not hear is the prayer for selfish things or desires. Look at James 4:3; "Ye ask, and receive not, because ye ask amiss, that ye may consume it upon your lusts." I believe God wants us to pray for material things only rarely. A good principle is to *pray* for spiritual things and *work* for material things.

Many folks sit around all their lives, eight hours a day, blaming God for letting them down. God knows you have a back and muscles. He made us to work and labor. I know people who have nice possessions, but they have usually paid the price in education, in labor, or in both. God wants us to labor for material things. Now, God does bless us in meeting our needs. God has blessed me in many unexpected ways such as a ten-dollar bill, a car payment, a house payment through my years of college and seminary. But those things came so I could be the instrument of God to fulfill the responsibilities God had for my life. If we pray for selfish reasons, God says he will not hear that prayer.

The Bible states that God will give the "desires of thine heart" (Ps. 37:4). It also says we can be filled with the Holy Spirit. But just like there are conditions to being filled with the Holy Spirit, there are conditions that must be met in order to receive the desires of our heart, and one is that we desire the things that will ultimately benefit the kingdom of God. God will not hear the selfish prayer of a person who repeats, "I want, I want. God, gimmee, gimmee." God doesn't want that kind of prayer.

My wife, Sandy, and I had the opportunity to eat dinner with Dr. and Mrs. W. A. Criswell, of the First Baptist Church of Dallas. In the conversation Dr. Criswell told us about an unusually exuberant and exciting Christian woman. Her little boy had asked for a rabbit. She said, "Son, we have two dogs, three cats, and 'a partridge in a pear tree.' We've got everything, and we don't need a rabbit. You cannot have a rabbit."

He said, "Mom, I've been studying about prayer, and I'm going to pray for a rabbit." She said, "Son, you just help yourself."

He began to pray for a rabbit. One Saturday he went to the movies and afterwards a magician performed. The magician pulled a rabbit out of his hat and did some other tricks.

Then the magician said, "I'm going to give this rabbit away. I am going to give it to a person who's nine rows back, five seats over." The little boy counted back nine rows and five seats over and found that it was his seat. He ran up there and yelled, "God answers prayer! God answers prayer." His mother said that he exclaimed all the way down the sidewalk after the show as the other children came to look at the rabbit, "God answers prayer!" God does answer prayer like that sometimes, but he always checks the motives first.

There's not a person in America who has less than some of the people who wrote the Bible. Of course, David, Solomon, and Sheba are some of the exceptions. Yet, you will not find much sympathy in the Bible for your desires because all of us are wealthy in Christ. God is concerned that ultimately and finally his kingdom be blessed. Pray for those things that honor the church and the winning of souls to Jesus Christ.

Prayers Against God's People

Thirdly, God will not answer a prayer against his people. Some people pray against the works of God. Some people pray against a particular church. Some people have such a bad attitude toward a preacher that if he preaches and someone walks the aisle and makes a decision, it makes the individual mad because it might encourage the preacher and help validate his ministry. Some people, deep down in their hearts, pray, "Now, God, I don't want any good thing to happen to that church, to that preacher, to that music director. Bring something into the life of those people to straighten them up."

There was a man in the Bible, Haman, who built a gallows for someone, and guess whose it became? Beware when you pray for God to straighten someone else out. God may say, "Hey, Buddy, before you pray, how about you?"

God does not hear the prayer of one who tries to straighten someone else out in vengeance or in a vindictive spirit. God indicates, "I'll not hear that kind of prayer." There was a time in Numbers 22 when Balaam prayed, "O God, I want you to curse someone." And God said, "Balaam, I don't hear that kind of a prayer [even though Balaam was a prophet of God]. Balaam, I won't hear it."

There was a time when Saul prayed, "God, I want you to get David. I want David to be slain. I want David to be persecuted." God said to Saul, "You know better than that. I don't hear that kind of a prayer."

If someone does not want the church of Jesus Christ to prosper, or God's people to prosper, or God's messengers to prosper, they can pray until they are blue in the face, but God will not hear that prayer. God does not hear the prayers of those who pray for others to suffer disadvantages.

Some people have admitted that they pray for a particular football team to win a game. But God is not on anyone's side. God doesn't hear the prayer from that kind of heart.

Prayers from Unforgiving Spirits

The fourth prayer the Bible says God refuses to hear is the prayer of a person who has a grudge in his heart, or an unforgiving spirit.

Matthew 5:23-24 says, "Therefore if thou bring thy gift to the altar, and there rememberest that thy brother hath ought against thee: Leave there thy gift before the altar, and go thy way; first, be reconciled to thy brother, and then come and offer thy gift." We need offerings in the church, but God says, before you give that money, get things right with that person you've offended or who has offended you. God says before you even come to the altar to pray, first of all get things straightened out.

Before anything, God desires that a person be right with others, whether it is a business partner, employer, employee, husband, or whomever. Some have such rotten feelings about an ex-wife or ex-husband that God won't answer their prayers because there is so much hatred in their hearts.

God does not want you to hold a grudge or have an unforgiving spirit. If a person has accumulated problems with others, that person has just that many problems with Jesus. Jesus said, "Inasmuch as ye have done it unto one of the least of these my brethren, ye have done it unto me" (Matt. 25:40). God will not answer the prayer of those with a grudge.

Prayers from Unclean Hearts

Next, God will not answer the prayer of those with unconfessed sins in their lives. In Psalm 66:18 the Psalmist writes, "If I regard iniquity in my heat, the

Lord will not hear me." Iniquity means sin. It means if I entertain sin consistently in my life, God will not hear my prayer. The first prayer anyone ought to pray is, "God, I confess my sin to you." Some say, "I've got some sins in my life, but that's not what I want God to solve. I've got some sins in my life, but I'm praying for some other things." Those are wasted prayers! If someone has a passel of big, ugly sins in his life, but only wants God to forgive the little sins, God will not answer that person.

Imagine a man coming to his wife and saying, "Honey, I want to apologize because back in 1971 I lied to you. Do you remember when you asked me if I'd mailed the letters? Honey, I told you I had. Well, they're still on the visor in the car, and I want to apologize to you." All the time the wife knows, while he is apologizing for what he did in 1971, he is having flirtations down at the office, and occasionally even commits adultery. He has lied to her, and thinks because he's apologized for one lie, it's totally going to solve all their marital problems. To confess that little pet sin, but to fail to confess the multitude of major sins, means that God will not hear that confession.

God wants us to clean house. He wants us to clean out the channel. He wants his Spirit to be able to flow through us, and that cannot happen as long as it is clogged up with sin. Many of us have confessed over and over. Some may give up alcohol one time and pray, "Oh, God, thank you for making me perfect. I gave up alcohol." But what if there are many areas God still wants in your life? God said he cannot hear the prayers of those with iniquity in their hearts.

God always sees us coming boldly into his throne room. But what often happens when we come into the throne room of God? We come with a bunch of old garbage and try to hide it. We say, "God, I want to ask you . . . ."

And God says, "Would you turn loose of that habit?"

"No, God."

"Would you turn loose of that attitude?

"No, God, did you see that? God, you can't see it now, can you? God, I'll hide it in my shirt pocket. God, I'll hide it in the back of my car. God, I want to pray about . . . ."

But God asks, "How about those sins?"When we come into the throne room with a load of ugly vicious sins, God says, "I cannot hear your prayers."

What do you think would happen if I were asked to perform a wedding ceremony, and I came up to the church without having shaved in two weeks, wearing a pair of clodhoppers, muddy jeans, and a sweaty T-shirt? Can't you see me walking into the sanctuary and asking "Where's your daughter? Let's get on with this wedding."

I wouldn't come to perform a wedding in my old garden shoes and with dirty fingernails, matted hair, and filthy, smelly clothes! But many of us go into God's throne room covered in dirt! Dirty! God indicates, "When you come dirty like that, I'll not hear your prayers." Your first prayer must be, "God, clean me up. I confess all those sins to you right now."

Prayers from Hypocritical Family Relationships

There's a sixth prayer the Bible says God will not answer. Look in 1 Peter 3:7. "Likewise, ye husbands, dwell with them according to knowledge, giving honour unto the wife, as unto the weaker vessel, and as being heirs together of the grace of life; that your prayers be not hindered." The word *hindered* literally means blocked. God wants there to be no obstacle to your prayers.

I'm amazed when people come to me and say, "Preacher, we're like lovebirds at church, but when we get home it's a different matter. When we get to church, it's blessings and Beatitudes, but when we get home, it's bickering and bedlam." What a horrible thing! The Bible says, "Let not the sun go down upon your wrath" (Eph. 4:26).

I counseled with a couple sometime ago. The man would come home from work every day and say, "Fill up my plate." She'd fill up his plate and he'd take it, leave the children, go to his bedroom, put his plate on a TV tray, and watch television without spending any more time with his family.

I asked the wife, "How long has he done that?" She said, "Ever since we were married. He doesn't eat with me and the kids. He just comes home, puts a full plate on his tray, and watches television in his bedroom with the door shut to keep us out. What would you do?" I said, "Dump his plate in his lap." That may not be remarkable spiritual advice, but that's what I would do. It probably wouldn't solve the problem. But if that is his attitude at home toward his wife and family, that man is a big, fat hypocrite. If what a man has doesn't work at home, it won't work anywhere. God does not want bitter family strife. God will not hear the prayers of a person like that.

Clean out the channels and watch God begin to work. We need to be prayer warriors: pure, holy, and righteous before God. We must be that kind of people.

In Glendale, Arizona, some boys tried to witness to Ricky. Ricky was a vile, mean, cussing, pot-smoking boy they'd brought to a Christian camp with them. They prayed for him, but all through the week he never moved toward Christ. On the last night of that Christian camp, Ricky walked the aisle and gave his heart and life to Christ.

That night, in the cabin, the three boys who had been praying for Ricky began to talk. At that camp they had an honor system at the concession stand. There was some candy, and a little cardboard box to put money in when you got a candy bar. One boy who'd been praying for Ricky said, "Man, I've just got to tell you guys something. I've been taking candy that costs a quarter out of the box, and I've been putting in a dime. I went out in the woods today, and I confessed, and I believe that's why God honored my prayers and Ricky got saved."

Another boy said, "You know what, I've been going to the candy stand and getting out a candy bar that costs a quarter, and I've been putting in a nickel. I went out in the woods tonight, and I prayed and confessed."

The third boy who had been praying all week said, "Guys, I just love those candy bars, and I've been getting them two or three at a time and putting them in my pockets without putting any money in the box. I went out in the woods and prayed, and not only did I confess, but I went to that cardboard box and put all my money into it and said, "God, I hope that's enough, because it's all I have.' " Those three boys had confessed their sins, gotten right with God, and their prayers were honored. And Ricky was saved.

There is one prayer God loves to hear. "Lord, be merciful to me a sinner, and save me for Christ's sake." He wants to hear that prayer from the heart of every lost woman, man, boy, and girl. God will hear anyone who will say, "God, I'm a lost, undone sinner, and I want to be born again." God will not refuse to hear that prayer.

We must be certain to remember that a person has no claim at all on the privilege of access to the presence of God when he is outside of God's Son, Jesus Christ. Be saved today, and appropriate God's riches through prayer as one who is joined to Jesus.